# GIS for Everyone

## Third Edition

Exploring your neighborhood and your world
with a Geographic Information System

*David E. Davis*

ESRI PRESS
REDLANDS, CALIFORNIA

ESRI
    GIS for Everyone
    ISBN 1-879102-91-9

First edition June 1999. Second edition November 2000. Third edition February 2003.

Printed in the United States of America.

*Library of Congress Cataloging-in-Publication Data*
Davis, David E. (David Edward), 1966–
    GIS for everyone : exploring your neighborhood and your world with a geographic information system / David E. Davis. —3d ed.
        p.   cm.
    ISBN 1-58948-056-2
    1. Geographic information systems  I. Title.
G70.212.D383 2003
910'.285—dc21                                        2003001729

Published by ESRI, 380 New York Street, Redlands, California 92373-8100.

Books from ESRI Press are available to resellers worldwide through Independent Publishers Group (IPG). For information on volume discounts, or to place an order, call IPG at 1-800-888-4741 in the United States, or at 312-337-0747 outside the United States.

# CONTENTS

*v*

# ACKNOWLEDGMENTS

THIS BOOK could not have been written without the cooperation of the organizations that shared their data for the explorations, Map Gallery, and sample data on the CD.

The San Diego Association of Governments (SANDAG) provided most of the data for exploration 2. Other San Diego data layers can be downloaded from the SANDAG Web site at *www.sandag.cog.ca.us.*

Titan Systems Corporation provided its Sure!MAPS® RASTER topographic map data for San Diego and samples on the CD. You can visit their Web page at *www.suremaps.com.*

Geographic Data Technology, Inc. (GDT), provided the data for Washington, D.C., Rio de Janeiro, and Austin. You can download several GDT layers with the special access code inside the back cover of this book and visit the GDT Web site at *www.geographic.com.*

The Institute of Municipal Informatics of Capital Prague provided all the background data for exploration 4-2 such as streets, parcels, and water. ARCDATA PRAGUE provided the restaurant and attractions themes used in the same exploration. Special thanks to Jan Vodnansky and Petr Seidl. You can visit their Web site at *www.arcdata.cz.*

The Texas Natural Resources Information System (TNRIS), a division of the Texas Water Development Board, provided the aerial image of Austin and several other data layers used in exploration 5-1. Special thanks to Gordon Wells. You can access and download digital geographic data for Texas at the TNRIS Web site at *www.tnris.state.tx.us.*

Special thanks to Jack Dangermond, president of ESRI, for his societal GIS vision and desire to bring GIS to everyone.

Next, I thank Bill Miller and Judy Boyd for allowing me to write this book and providing the best support imaginable. Christian Harder, manager of ESRI Press, gave me his enthusiasm and trust and led me through the book-publishing process.

And to all my colleagues in the Educational Products department, thank you for generously sharing your time and professional experience throughout the project.

Thanks to R.W. Greene and Michael Karman for carefully editing each page of the manuscript. Your contributions to the book are invaluable.

Michael Hyatt designed the book and did page production, copyediting, and proofreading. Steve Pablo designed and produced the cover. Barbara Shaeffer-Smith reviewed the text from a legal perspective.

My sincere thanks to Deane Kensok for his many ideas and for the hard work he put into this project, including obtaining data and permissions.

Judy Boyd, Mike Tait, Deane Kensok, Charlie Fitzpatrick, and Michael Phoenix read drafts of the book and provided excellent comments.

Dan Primavera of ESRI BIS provided updated demographic data for the Washington, D.C., and New York explorations.

Bjorn Svensson and Ginger McKay worked on the EDU_Sequoia map service for the sequoia groves exploration.

Thanks to El-Can Exploration, Inc., of Spring, Texas, for countless consultations during the creation of the sequoia groves exploration.

# INTRODUCTION

THERE'S GOOD REASON why the period we live in is often referred to as an Information Age—the exchange of information, especially digital information, has become the critical ingredient for success in any activity. It seems inconceivable, in this age, to conduct any kind of business without using technological tools such a personal computer, without sending communication by e-mail, without accessing the Internet. Using and exchanging information in digital form has now become practically essential for the most routine activities: applying for a new job, looking for a new home, researching new markets for business, measuring the impact of a government policy, finding information for a project—or even for making plans to get away from all of that and go on vacation.

A specific kind of digital information has also become essential for these myriad activities: geographic information.

Although we tend not to think about it much, it's a plain fact that everything human beings do takes place at a particular location on the earth: every activity, thing, trend, issue, or phenomenon has a geographic component to it. In the routine activities listed above, the question "where" is a crucial part of the larger issue: if that issue concerns a job offer, the location of that new job will be vital to whether you accept the offer or not. If the issue concerns a certain public policy, legislators are all too aware that the people affected live—and vote—in specific geographic areas. If that issue concerns finding a new place to live, you need only refer to the real-estate agent's Three Most Important Criteria for a buying a new home: location, location, location.

In fact, when larger issues such as these are considered with reference to where they are taking place in the world, the larger issue is often transformed. Most of the time, when viewed through geographic lenses, an issue can be seen with an astonishing new clarity.

The digital revolution of the late twentieth century has allowed this kind of geographic information to be more easily accessed than ever before. Using geographic information systems—GIS—organizations are now able to analyze issues and opportunities and to solve problems and conflicts across a huge range of subjects. GIS, a technology only about thirty years old, has become for many organizations, including public, private, for-profit, and nonprofit, as essential for decision making and analysis as e-mail and broadband access.

GIS works by linking information—data—to a geographic location. We tend to think of geography traditionally in terms of the physical attributes of a land mass—how high mountains are, where rivers flow, how many people live within the boundaries of an administrative area. In reality, geography is much more than this. The power of GIS lies in the fact that using computer technology, any conceivable kind of information can be linked to any geographic location. In a GIS, maps become supermaps. When you look at a road on a traditional paper map, you learn roughly where it goes, and its name, and that's about all. Click on that same map in a GIS and you can find out how many lanes the road has, when it was built and by which construction company, the composition of the road surface, how much it cost the taxpayers to build, and when the potholes in it are scheduled to get filled.

This wealth of data is not limited to these kinds of physical attributes; it can include any information associated with the people who live in a particular location. Thus, a GIS can display maps of census and demographic information, for use by government institutions and marketers; maps of illnesses and health conditions, for use by doctors and hospitals; maps of crimes and crime patterns, for use by police and legislators; maps of areas prone to flooding or forest fires, for use by emergency services personnel. There is virtually no limit to the type and amount of information that can be associated with a particular place in a GIS.

The other power of GIS lies in the way it lets its users layer several different kinds of information on top of each other about the same location, much like a baker places layers on a cake. This allows comparisons and analyses to be made, in turn revealing causes and effects that might never have been discovered by a traditional quantitative analysis. A layer of information about illnesses in a particular area can be compared to another information layer showing toxic chemical storage sites—giving public health officials clues about how to stop the illness. A layer of information about educational attainment and income level can be compared to a layer of available retail locations—helping business owners with expansion plans. A layer of information about crime locations can be compared with a layer showing police patrol patterns—giving law enforcement officials a new tool for redeployment decisions.

In earlier years, GIS users needed a lot of computer firepower to create these kinds of decision-making tools. But the digital revolution is bringing these tools to anyone who wants to use them. Interactive Web sites that allow you to create your own GIS maps and to do your own GIS analysis are popping up everywhere. At many sites, such as ESRI's Geography Network℠, diverse kinds of geographic information have been consolidated into one Web portal—where you can can view static maps, or download geographic data for your own GIS projects, or stream real-time geographic data into your PC.

GIS is now for everyone: for students creating projects in school or college, for neighborhood groups and activists, or for anyone with just a desire to know more about what's really in the world around them.

*GIS for Everyone* is intended to be an easy-to-use, easy-to-understand intro-duction to this rich world of digital geographic information. Using the free software and data supplied on the CD that comes with this book, and fol-lowing the simple exercises, you can teach yourself the basics of layering information in a GIS, organizing and presenting GIS maps, and finding data for your own projects. You will learn about the different ways that various organizations are using GIS data, how that data is formatted, and the best ways data can be used for your purposes. Each reader will be able to down-load geographic data for his or her own area, and to download additional geographic data from the Geography Network. By the end of the book, you'll be able to create stunning digital maps for just about any purpose you can think of, using data from anywhere in the world.

We hope that will allow you to join not just the Information Age, but the Geographic Information Age.

# CHAPTER 1

# Varieties of GIS experience

IF YOU'RE STILL THINKING that geography consists of boring maps of mountains and roads, this chapter is intended to convince you otherwise, as we present a small sample of the enormous variety of maps and geographic analysis that are being created every day using GIS technology.

# Map Gallery

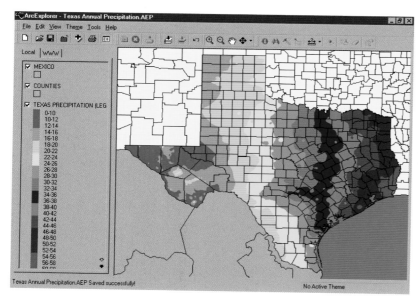

GIS can provide visual explanations of phenomena that work better than rows of numbers might. This simple ArcExplorer™ project, using data downloaded from the Oregon Climate Service at Oregon State University (ocs.orst.edu), shows vividly how the state of Texas gets noticeably wetter going from west to east.

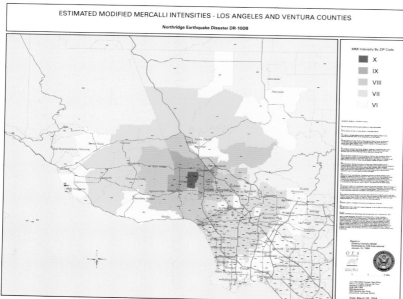

In emergency and disaster situations, GIS is becoming a valuable tool for helping people. This GIS earthquake map from the 1994 Northridge earthquake in Los Angeles, created by the California Governor's Office of Emergency Services, was used for directing assistance payments to people whose homes were damaged. Those residents who lived within areas identified as having suffered damage at VIII or above on the Mercalli index (an earthquake damage scale) were approved for expedited assistance, and did not have to jump through the usual bureaucratic hoops to receive help fast.

*Varieties of GIS experience*

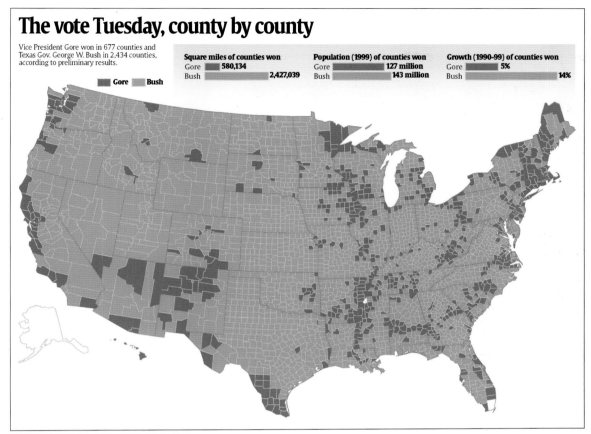

# The vote Tuesday, county by county

Vice President Gore won in 677 counties and
Texas Gov. George W. Bush in 2,434 counties,
according to preliminary results.

Gore    Bush

**Square miles of counties won**
Gore — 580,134
Bush — 2,427,039

**Population (1999) of counties won**
Gore — 127 million
Bush — 143 million

**Growth (1990-99) of counties won**
Gore — 5%
Bush — 14%

*Journalists have begun to take advantage of the speed and visual power of GIS. This map showing the majority vote for president in November 2000 for every U.S. county was created in MapShop, a joint venture of the Associated Press and ESRI®. The morning after the election, it gave American news readers an immediate, graphic portrait of the new political geography of the nation.*

Varieties of GIS experience

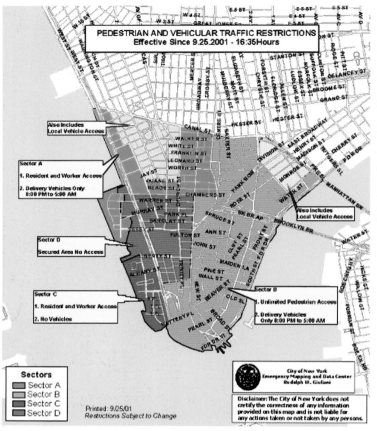

GIS specialists and digital cartographers were an integral part of the recovery efforts after the September 11 attacks on New York City and Washington, D.C. They supplied a huge array of maps to rescue workers and officials, including maps of the underground hazards at the World Trade Center, maps of the massive debris pile itself, and maps like this one informing the public which areas of lower Manhattan were accessible and which were off limits. These maps changed hourly and daily in the early weeks of the disaster, to keep up with the fast past of changing conditions.

Topographic maps like this one of Highland in Southern California show natural surface features of a geographic area, and are most useful for hiking and camping, or for siting new buildings. The most detailed of these are created by the United States Geological Survey (USGS) at 1:24,000 scale for the entire United States. They can be scanned and imported into a GIS where they are useful as detailed basemaps. This specific map is from National Geographic's TOPO! Series, available for preview and purchase from the Geography Network, www.geographynetwork.com.

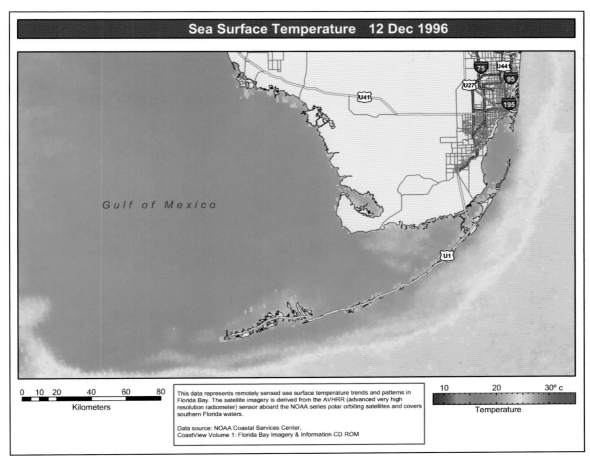

GIS is not only useful in dealing with ground surface features of the earth, it has also found wide application in oceanographic and other marine applications. This map shows a satellite image of sea surface temperature off the coast of south Florida. The data used to construct this map was obtained with an AVHRR (Advanced Very High Resolution Radiometer) sensor carried on one of the satellites operated by NOAA, the National Oceanic and Atmospheric Administration. On this map, green represents cooler water, while yellow and orange represent warmer. Maps such as these can help in studies of ocean current flow, distribution of sea life, global energy budgeting, and weather and climatological trends such as El Niño and La Niña.

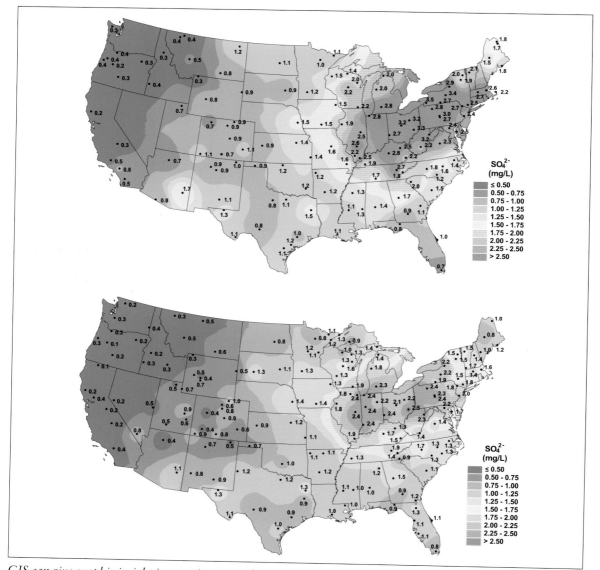

GIS can give graphic insight into environmental trends and the effect of environmental policies, making it much easier for legislators and the public to understand what exactly is going on in the physical world. These two maps from the National Atmospheric Deposition Program show the effects of acid rain in 1985 and 1998. Acid rain has mainly afflicted northeastern states that are downwind from older power plants located in midwest states; pollutants from these plants are carried aloft and then fall in rain, depositing sulfates on the ground. These maps show concentrations of these sulfates in the two years, and show a noticeable change, although much work still needs to be done. Much of the reduction is attributable to the regulations of the Clean Air Act.

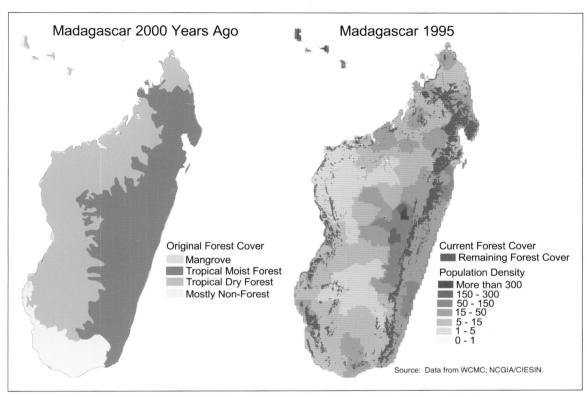

*Changes in the natural world over extended periods of time can be visualized in a GIS, helping measure the long-term effects of one phenomenon, such as human civilization, on another. These maps of the island of Madagascar, courtesy of Population Action International, provide striking evidence of the extent of deforestation. One of the most biologically rich and unique spots on earth (home to 5 percent of the world's species), Madagascar is in danger of becoming one of the poorest biologically. All but 10 percent of the forests have been burned, replaced mainly by coffee plantations, cattle ranches, and mining operations. A booming population, mass migration to cities, and hard economic times have also had a deleterious effect on the island's natural existence.*

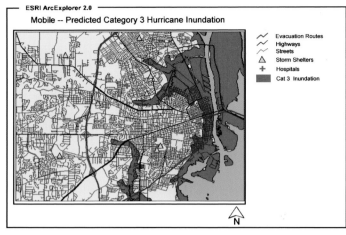

This map of Mobile, Alabama, shows the area forecasters say could be in danger from the storm surge of a category 3 hurricane. Data is from the NOAA Coastal Services Center, Charleston, South Carolina.

Geography is an intrinsic element of many outdoor sports, so GIS is finding wide application in a variety of tourist and recreational applications. This map, courtesy of Clover Point Cartographics Ltd. of Victoria, B.C., and Canadian Mountain Holidays Ltd., shows in graphic detail the heli-ski runs in the Canadian Rockies near the town of Revelstoke available for the adventurous.

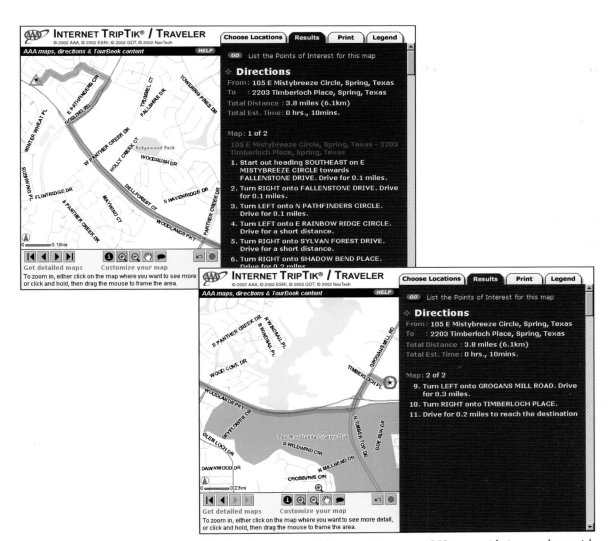

The American Automobile Association uses GIS to provide its members with an Internet-based driving-direction and vacation-planning service. Called AAA Internet TripTik®/Traveler, the system allows any AAA member to go online, type in an origin point and destination, and then access a digital map with a direct route to the destination. Included is travel information not only for the destination, but for points all along the route itself—scenic roads, points of interest, gas stations, restaurants, lodging, campgrounds, AAA-approved auto repair locations, detour and construction information, and bridge and ferry information, all of it in an easy-to-follow, tiled map format. The system is powered by ArcIMS® and produces more than six million maps per month. It is available to AAA members from www.aaa.com.

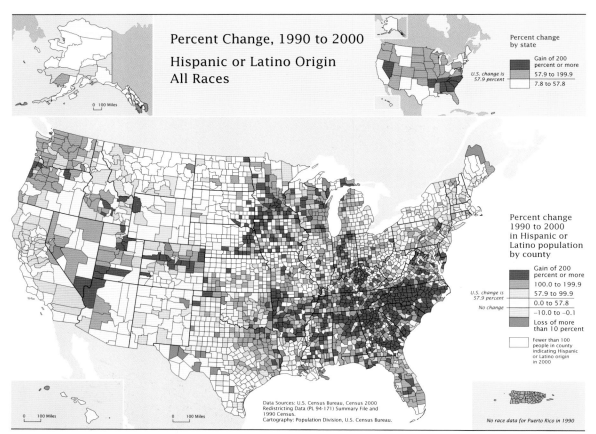

Percent Change, 1990 to 2000

Hispanic or Latino Origin
All Races

Percent change by state

Gain of 200 percent or more

57.9 to 199.9

7.8 to 57.8

U.S. change is 57.9 percent

Percent change 1990 to 2000 in Hispanic or Latino population by county

Gain of 200 percent or more

100.0 to 199.9

57.9 to 99.9

0.0 to 57.8

−10.0 to −0.1

Loss of more than 10 percent

Fewer than 100 people in county indicating Hispanic or Latino origin in 2000

U.S. change is 57.9 percent

No change

Data Sources: U.S. Census Bureau, Census 2000 Redistricting Data (PL 94-171) Summary File and 1990 Census.
Cartography: Population Division, U.S. Census Bureau.

No race data for Puerto Rico in 1990

*Census data is a rich source of information about the population of the United States, and is easily incorporated into a GIS. It can create some striking portraits of the nation in human terms. This map, from* Mapping Census 2000: The Geography of U.S. Diversity *(ESRI Press 2001) shows vividly the speed and direction of the migration of persons of Hispanic origin in a ten-year period.*

# CHAPTER 2

# Understanding digital maps

ANYONE CAN USE A PAPER MAP. All you need to do is unfold it, and spread out before you is a colorful representation of cities and roads, mountains and rivers, railroads and boundary lines. The cities are represented by small circles, roads by black lines, and lakes by small blue areas similar in shape to the real lakes.

Up on a computer monitor, a digital map looks much the same. As on the paper map, there are points that represent features on the map such as cities; there are lines that represent linear features such as roads, and small areas that represent area features such as lakes.

But in a digital map, additional information—about where the point is, and how long the road is, or how many square miles the lake occupies—is stored in digital format, in a file or database. You can access this additional information when you want it simply by clicking on that spot on the digital map.

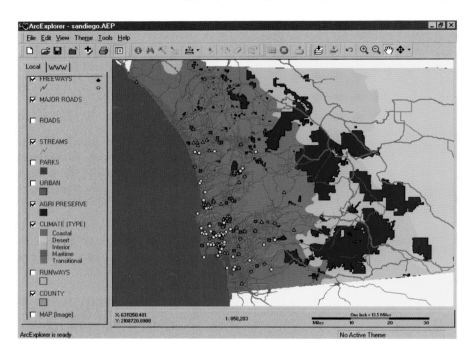

It's helpful to think of the digital geographic data as layers of information that you can turn on or off, depending on your task. These layers are called themes, and each theme represents a type of feature of the area you're looking at. For example, a theme of roads would contain all the information you have available about all the roads in a particular area—their locations, names, lengths, and who has jurisdiction over them, for example. Another theme might represent all the lakes in the same area. Still another could represent all the cities. Each theme can be turned on or off, making all the elements of the theme—the roads, cities, or lakes—appear or disappear, with the touch of a key.

These themes can be laid on top of one another, creating a stack of information about the same geographic area. Turning a theme off or on is like placing a layer on the stack, or peeling it off. By turning layers on and off, you control the amount of information about an area that you want to see. If you turn off all the layers, you'll get a blank screen. Next, you can turn on a basemap, at the bottom of the pile of layers—this might show only the familiar physical geography of the area, or perhaps political and administrative boundaries. On top of this basemap, you could then place a theme of cities, then a theme of roads, then one of fire stations, then one of railroads, then one of historic places—and so forth. Each of these layers is transparent, so that you can continue to see the layers beneath. By the time you're done stacking layers, you'd end up with a map on your computer screen that pretty much matches the paper map, except that in the digital map, you also have instantaneous access to all the information available about each individual feature.

ArcExplorer, the software used to create the maps in chapter 1, is included on the companion CD. Once you install it, we'll proceed to explore some geographic features and themes in San Diego, California.

### INSTALL ARCEXPLORER 2

To run ArcExplorer, you must have Microsoft® Windows® 98, Windows 2000, Windows NT® version 4.0, or Windows XP installed on your system. If you're running Windows NT, you must have Service Pack 3, 4, 5, or 6a installed.

To install ArcExplorer,

1  Insert the *GIS for Everyone* CD in your CD–ROM drive.

2  Choose Run from the Start menu.

3  In the Command Line box, type the path **Software\ArcExplorer2** and the file name **AESetup.exe** (for example, **E:\Software\ArcExplorer2\AESetup.exe**).

4  When asked which components to install, choose all of them:

◆ Application Files: The core of ArcExplorer software.

◆ Help and Tutorial Files: Online help system and an ArcExplorer manual in PDF format (aemanual.pdf).

◆ Web Integration Tools: The World Wide Web (WWW) functionality of ArcExplorer. These tools allow you to view and download data from the Web using ArcExplorer.

The setup program will automatically install ArcExplorer on your PC and place a shortcut to start the program on your desktop.

You'll find an ArcExplorer toolbar reference page at the back of this book.

# Exploration 2   Look at San Diego

In this first exploration you see a paper map, from the United States Geological Survey, that's been scanned into the computer. On it, you can find the San Diego Zoo, the airport, and Sea World, just as you would with a paper map. You'll look at the same area on a digital map to get your first taste of how these things are represented as layers of digital geographic data.

**ArcExplorer**

1   Start ArcExplorer either by double-clicking the ArcExplorer shortcut on your desktop or by selecting Programs:ESRI:ArcExplorer from the Start menu. You'll see the ArcExplorer opening banner, then the ArcExplorer window.

**2**   Click the Open Project button. In the dialog box that displays, navigate to the *explore\sandiego* directory on the CD.

**3**   Select the project file called *sandiego.AEP* and click Open. (The AEP extension stands for ArcExplorer Project.) Project files store all the work you do with ArcExplorer. They contain the paths to the data and information about how it's displayed.

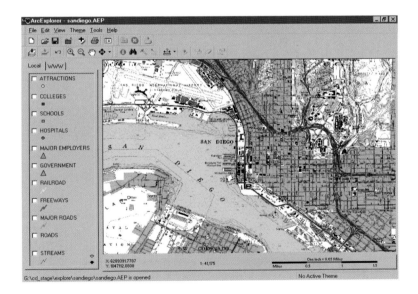

In the map view is a scanned paper map of San Diego. It shows such features as elevation, highways, streets, parks, buildings, airports, and bodies of water. Scanned maps are excellent visual backdrops for other geographic data. Although you can learn a lot from a paper map, the amount of information you can get from it is limited to what's shown, and you can't exclude things you may not need to see.

In ArcExplorer, each layer of digital data—the theme—is listed to the left of the map view in what is called the legend. The map view of San Diego contains a theme for streets, one for highways, another for parks, as well as additional themes for major attractions, hospitals, and other features of life in San Diego.

4  Use the down arrow at the bottom of the legend to scroll down. In the legend, turn off the "paper" map by unchecking the box next to the MAP theme. This turns off the view of the scanned paper map. Turn on the RAILROAD, FREEWAYS, MAJOR ROADS, ROADS, PARKS, RUNWAYS, and COUNTY themes by checking the boxes.

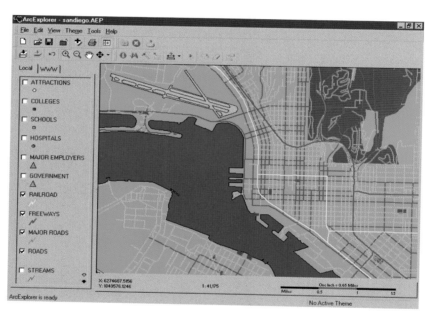

This looks familiar. But in this digital map view of San Diego, you can look at different features and combinations of features in the area by turning themes on and off. Moreover, in the digital map, you can perform particular operations on a theme by making it "active." You do this by clicking on its name in the legend. When it's made active, the theme will appear to be raised above the surface of the legend, and you'll see its name at the bottom right of the ArcExplorer screen.

5   Turn on the ATTRACTIONS, COLLEGES, SCHOOLS, HOSPITALS, MAJOR EMPLOYERS, and GOVERNMENT themes by checking their boxes in the legend. Suddenly, a bunch of squares, circles, and triangles appear, each representing a different theme.

6   Click on the name ATTRACTIONS in the legend to make the theme active. This makes additional operations with the theme possible.

7   Move your mouse pointer over some of the yellow circles. Because the theme is active, the name of the attraction will appear above the circle when you pass the pointer over it. See if you can find the San Diego Zoo, which is in a large park near the upper right of the map view. In the graphic below, we've found San Diego's international airport, also known as Lindbergh Field.

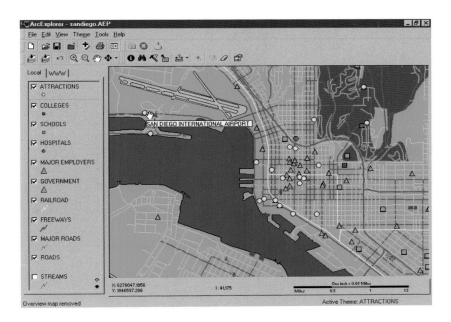

Try exploring some other themes. Click a theme name to make it active. You have the choice of HOSPITALS (red circles), GOVERNMENT (orange triangles), COLLEGES (blue squares), SCHOOLS (orange squares), or MAJOR EMPLOYERS (light blue triangles). Move your mouse pointer over some features to see their names.

Now that you've identified some features, it's time to move around the map. First, you'll explore San Diego with the Direction button.

**8** Choose a direction using the down arrow at the right of the Direction button. An arrow appears on the button to indicate the direction you selected. Click the Direction button to move in that direction. Try out a couple of other directions as well. Don't forget to drag your mouse pointer over things you encounter along the way. (And don't forget to make the theme active.)

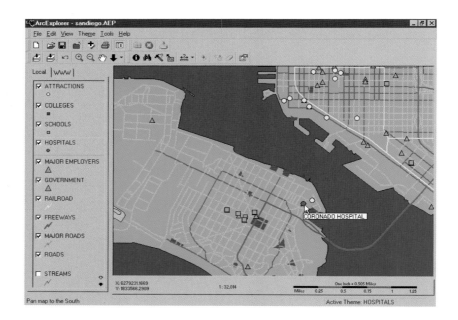

Notice that your map view changes in easy, controlled steps. Here you see that we panned south.

Try the Pan button. With it, you grab your display and drag it in any direction.

9   Click the Pan button. Move your mouse pointer into the map view, hold down the mouse button, and drag. When you get to where you want to be, release the button.

We're not sure where you'll end up in this exploration. Go ahead and move in any direction you want. In the graphic above, we panned to the northwest and ended up in the vicinity of Sea World.

Some themes represent features located all over the map; some represent features located in one area. In either case, you can zoom to the area covered by a particular theme. To see the whole map, the area covered by all the themes, you can click the Zoom to Full Extent button. Or you can zoom to the active theme with the Zoom to Active Theme button. And of course you can zoom in and out. Don't worry if you get lost. That Zoom to Full Extent button will bring you back to a view of the entire map.

**10** Click the Zoom In button. Click once somewhere in the map view to zoom in on that area. Click again to zoom in even more. You can also drag a box over an area to zoom in on it, as shown here.

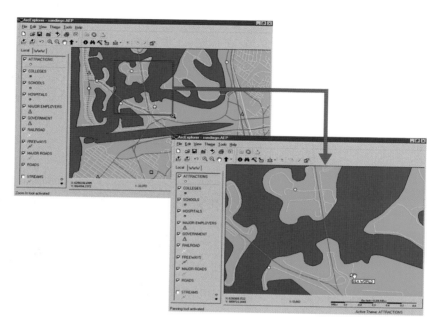

**11** Click the Zoom Out button. Click once somewhere in the map view to zoom out from that location. Click the Zoom Out button once more.

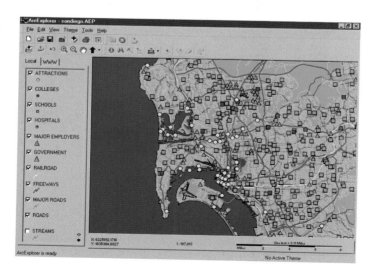

It's neither practical nor possible to include all the information about a place on a single map. So navigating in a digital map goes beyond zooming and panning with what you see. You have access to several different maps of the same place, and you can get to them as you navigate.

**12**  Turn off all themes except COUNTY.

**13**  Zoom to the extent of the COUNTY theme. (Make that theme active by clicking on its name, then use the Zoom to Active Theme button.)

Now you see all of San Diego County. The city of San Diego is a coastal town, but the much larger county is mostly farmland, with the glamorous avocado a specialty.

**14**  Turn on the AGRI PRESERVE theme.

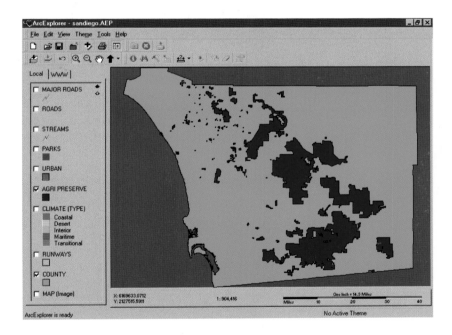

What about the climate for all that agriculture?

**15** Turn on the CLIMATE theme. You can see how many climate zones the county has, from the cool coastal climates in the west, to the hot, dry desert climates farther east.

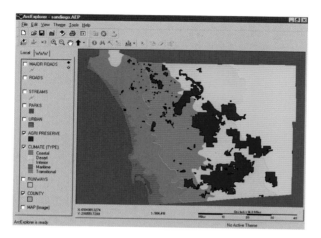

Perhaps now you're wondering what other effects the climate has.

**16** Turn off the AGRI PRESERVE theme. Turn on the URBAN theme. Just like that, you've changed the subject of your map. And you can see that most people would rather live along the coast than in the desert. Housing prices reflect that, although that's not a theme here.

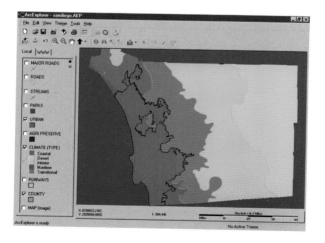

**17** Click the Close Project button. Choose No when asked if you want to save any changes.

# Finding answers with digital maps

Now that you've seen how layers of geographic information form a basic architecture of GIS technology, it's time to dig a little deeper. Huge amounts of information can exist in a GIS—those in use by governments and other large organizations can encompass thousands of terabytes of data—so it's critically important to know how to drill down into all those layers to find the exact pieces of information that you need.

First, it must be clear to you what that information is; you must refine your geographic questions. This is not necessarily a complex task, and in fact, everyone asks such questions every day. If, for example, you had found a better job in a new city and were preparing to move your family there, you'd be asking yourself all kinds of specific geographic questions: What are the neighborhoods like? Can we afford a house in a nice neighborhood? Where are housing prices rising or falling? How far will I have to commute? Which schools are the best? Are there parks or other open space nearby available for recreation?

Those layers in a GIS help answer such questions because layers are actually made up of two kinds of information about each geographic feature—its location on the planet, and a description of the feature itself.

The files that store location are the ones that allow you to see the features on the computer monitor, and which locate it accurately in relationship to other features and in the real world. Descriptions of features are known as attributes, and are stored in tables. These can be as numerous and complex as you want them to be, and they are what give a GIS its power.

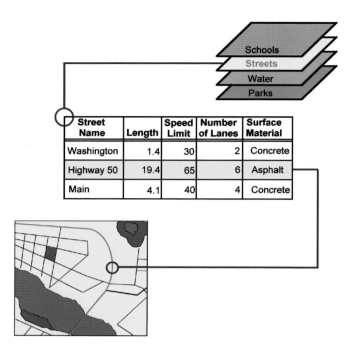

| Street Name | Length | Speed Limit | Number of Lanes | Surface Material |
|---|---|---|---|---|
| Washington | 1.4 | 30 | 2 | Concrete |
| Highway 50 | 19.4 | 65 | 6 | Asphalt |
| Main | 4.1 | 40 | 4 | Concrete |

In this chapter we'll see how ArcExplorer is able to access the large amounts of information in attribute tables, and the variety of ways the software is able to display the answers you're looking for.

Exploration 3-1   What is that?                                           Chapter 3

Finding answers with digital maps

# Exploration 3-1   What is that?

Back in San Diego, during exploration 2, you moved your mouse pointer over various features and saw their names pop up on your monitor. The tool that does this is called the MapTips tool. You can set the MapTips tool to read any of the attributes of a feature, because a feature's name is only one of many possible attributes.

1   The Washington, D.C., explorations require that the exploration data be copied to your local hard drive. Copy the *explore\dc* directory from the CD to your local hard disk, perhaps to your temp folder (for example, *C:\temp\dc*).

**ArcExplorer**

2   Start ArcExplorer, if necessary.

3   Click the Open Project button. In the dialog box that displays, navigate to the *dc* folder you just copied to your computer (for example, *C:\temp\dc*).

**4** Select the project file called *dc.AEP* and click Open. When the project opens, you see a map view of downtown Washington, D.C., with themes of landmarks, institutions, streets, water, parks, and census boundaries.

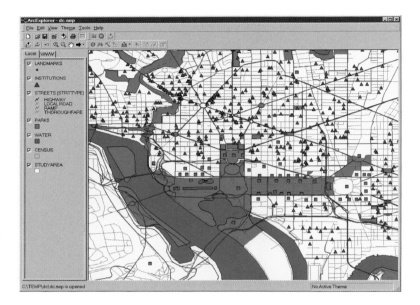

**5** Make the LANDMARKS theme active.

**6** Click on the MapTips tool. The MapTip Field Selection dialog box displays. This allows you to choose which attribute you want to pop up when you pass the mouse pointer over a particular element.

**7** Choose the *NAME* field and then click OK in the dialog box. The name of a particular landmark will appear when you pass your mouse pointer over it. It doesn't matter if the pointer is also set to do something else, like zooming in or panning. It will do both tasks.

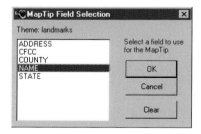

**8** Drag the mouse pointer over other landmarks and read their names.

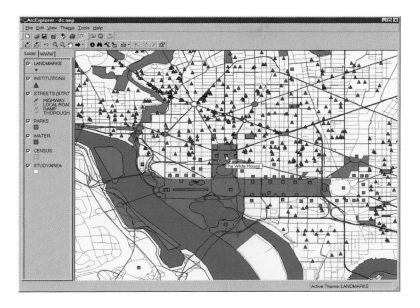

Changing the field you want to pop up is a simple matter.

**9** Click on the MapTips tool. Choose the *ADDRESS* field and then click OK in the dialog box.

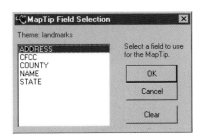

**10** Drag the mouse pointer over the landmarks. Now, the address or some kind of location information about each landmark appears.

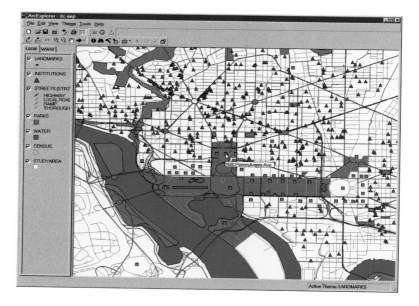

Another method of discovering information about a theme is to use the Identify tool.

**11** Turn off the INSTITUTIONS, LANDMARKS, and STREETS themes. Make the CENSUS theme active.

The CENSUS theme contains information about people—where they live, where they were born, how much they earn, what education level they attained, how old they are, how much rent they pay, their ethnicity. Census data is in fact one of the richest sources of information about the United States, and is easily accessible.

Census data is commonly divided into block groups, which are simply a collection of city blocks. You can use the Identify button to learn something about the people who live in various parts of Washington, D.C., from the census data of block groups.

**12** Click the Identify button. Now move your mouse pointer into the map view and click on some areas of the city at random.

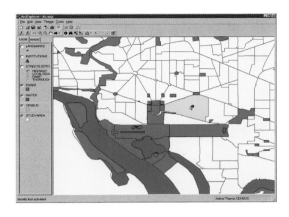

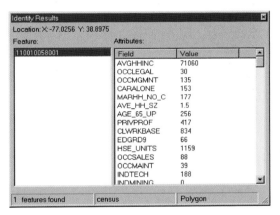

The first time you click on an area, the Identify Results dialog box will display. It lists all the attributes associated with the block group you clicked.

It's difficult to tell anything about the people of Washington, D.C., immediately. In fact, the entries in this box look like gibberish. They are, however, simply abbreviations that census takers have invented for various categories. For example, the entry *PRIVPROF* means "Employee of private, for-profit company." If you scroll down the list, you'll probably be able to figure out most of the others. For a full list of abbreviations translated into English, consult the file *CensusFieldDefinitions.htm* in the CD's *Explore* directory.

**13**  Close the Identify Results dialog box by clicking the ✕ in its upper right corner.

**14**  When you finish exploring the Census attributes, turn the INSTITUTIONS, LANDMARKS, and STREETS themes back on.

# Exploration 3-2   Where is it?

MapTips and Identify give you information about places you point to on the map. But sometimes you'll already have information about a place, and you want to find it on the map. To do this, you'll use the Find tool.

**1** Click the Find button. The Find Features dialog box displays.

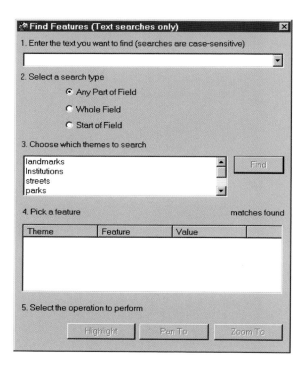

**2** Type **Smithsonian** in the text box. Note that the Find tool is case-sensitive, so be sure to enter the text exactly as shown.

**3** Since we didn't enter the full name of this famous museum—Smithsonian Institution—choose *Any Part of Field* in section 2 of the dialog box.

**4** Choose *LANDMARKS* as the theme to search in section 3.

**5** Click the Find button. ArcExplorer proceeds to search the features in the LANDMARKS theme and returns a list of matches.

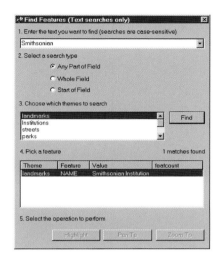

**6** Click on the match for the Smithsonian Institution to highlight it. You'll see that the Highlight, Pan To, and Zoom To buttons are no longer grayed out.

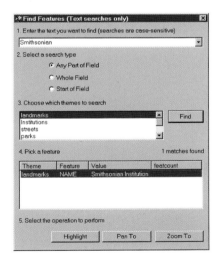

**7** Click the Highlight button. The point representing the Smithsonian on the map will be highlighted with a yellow triangle.

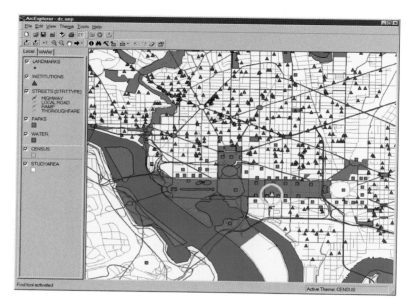

**8** Click the Zoom To button in the Find Features dialog box. You're zoomed in to the Smithsonian Institution and it's now in the center of the map view.

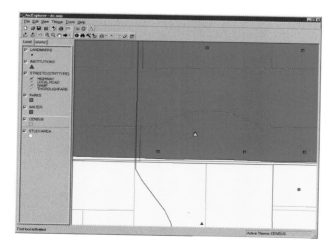

 **9** Click the Clear Selection button when you're finished viewing the location.

**10** Make the STUDYAREA theme active and click the Zoom to Active Theme button. You see the entire map—that is, the area covered by all the themes in the legend.

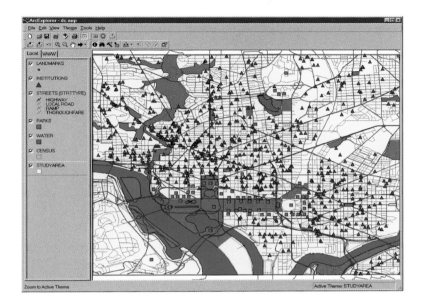

Like all of the tools you've used so far, the Find tool works with any theme.

**11** Type **CONSTITUTION GARDENS** as the text you want to find in the Find dialog box. (Be sure to enter the text in all capital letters.)

**12** Choose *Any Part of Field* as the search type.

**13** This time, choose the *PARKS* theme as the theme to search.

**14** Click Find.

**15**   Click on the match for Constitution Gardens.

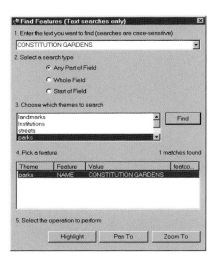

**16**   Use the Highlight button to highlight the park's location. Click the Zoom To button in the Find Features dialog box to zoom in on the park.

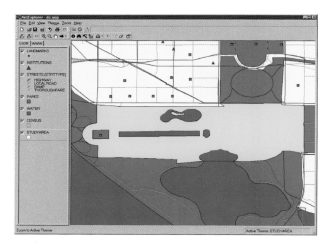

**17**   Close the Find Features dialog box.

   **18**   Click the Clear Selection button.

Exploration 3-3 How far is it? Chapter 3

Finding answers with digital maps

# Exploration 3-3  How far is it?

Now that you've gotten an idea of what's in the data, you're ready to perform some real geographic analysis, like using that data to measure distances.

1 Click the Zoom to Active Theme button.

2 Zoom in on the area shown in the red box below with the Zoom In tool.

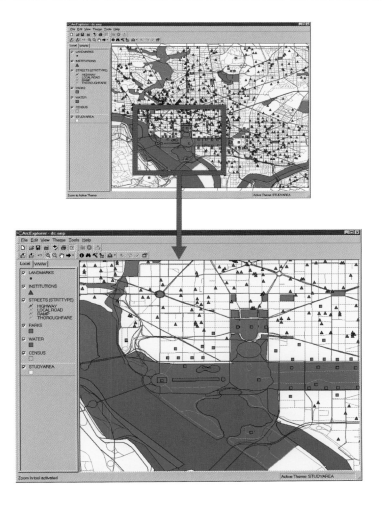

Finding distances is a two-step process. First, you must tell the GIS what kind of measurement units your map data is stored in. Second, you need to tell it which kind of measurement units you want it to use to tell you the distance.

The measurement units that map data is stored in are known as map units. Because there are so many different ways to collect and store data, it would be impossible for ArcExplorer to determine which map units were used in a project. To get an accurate measurement, you must tell ArcExplorer which map units your data is stored in. If you don't know the map units for your GIS data, check any accompanying documentation that came with the data, or ask the person who gave it to you. (If you can't find this information, you can zoom in on a familiar area and try all the possible map units until you get one that seems to provide the most accurate results. It would be better, of course, to obtain the map units from a reliable source.)

The ArcExplorer default map units are decimal degrees, and all of the Washington, D.C., themes use this default. Decimal degrees are degrees of latitude and longitude expressed as decimals rather than as degrees, minutes, and seconds. (For example, a point located at longitude 73 degrees, 59 minutes, and 15 seconds would be expressed as 73.9875 decimal degrees.) To use the Washington, D.C., data, you need only make sure that ArcExplorer is indeed set to decimal degrees.

As for the units you want ArcExplorer to use in telling you how far something is—the distance units—you can choose feet, miles, meters, or kilometers.

3   From the View menu, select Scale Bar Properties, then Map Units. Make sure that *Decimal Degrees* is checked. (If you use data that has different units, this is where you would tell ArcExplorer.)

4   Use the Find tool to locate the Lincoln Memorial, Washington Monument, and Jefferson Memorial if you don't know where they are. Dismiss the Find box after you've found them.

5   Click on the Measure tool down arrow, then choose *Miles* from the list. These are your distance units.

You can either measure distance between two points in a straight line or you can click several points along a route (at each turn) to get the total distance from start to finish.

First you'll measure the distance between the Lincoln Memorial to the Washington Monument.

**6** Click on the Measure tool (the pointer changes to a crosshair). Since the direct path between the two landmarks is through water, you'll need to measure the path in several segments. Click and hold the mouse as you drag a line segment from the center of the Lincoln Memorial toward the Washington Monument, avoiding the water. Release the mouse button at the end of your first segment.

The segment and total length you measured are displayed in the status panel at the top left of the map view.

Click and hold your mouse button again to complete your route to the Washington Monument. Release the mouse button at the end of each additional segment. Use as many segments as you need to measure the route.

The distance is about .8 miles from the Lincoln Memorial to the Washington Monument.

**7** Click and hold your mouse again as you drag more line segments from the center of the Washington Monument to the center of the Jefferson Memorial, avoiding the water.

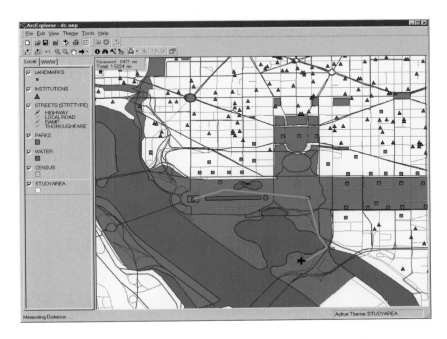

The total distance is about 1.5 miles.

If you want to measure the distance between more things, double-click any-where in your map view to begin a new measurement. After you double-click, the total length of your previous measurement, in this case the distance from the Lincoln Memorial to the Jefferson Memorial, appears in the lower left corner on the status bar.

Finding answers with digital maps

# Exploration 3-4   **What's it like?**

A third way of answering questions about an area is by using the Query Builder. As the name suggests, this tool helps you put together a question, the answer to which is shown on the map. This tool is especially suited to working with numeric attributes such as those found in census and demographic data. That data is commonly used by businesses to find customers.

Suppose, for example, that you wanted to open a small coffeehouse, specializing in boutique coffee drinks such as espresso and cappuccino. You'd want a location where people needed coffee. You'd also want a location where they could afford your high prices. You'd use the Query Builder to help you.

1   Click the Zoom to Full Extent button. You see the entire map—that is, the area covered by all the themes in the legend.

2   Turn off all of the themes except for the CENSUS theme. Make the CENSUS theme active.

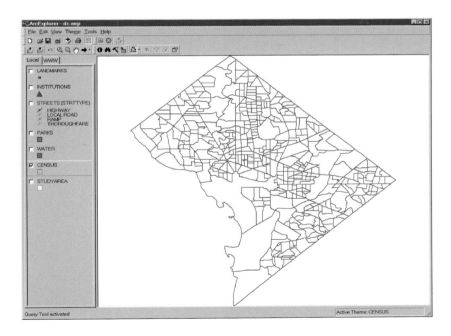

First, you need areas of the city where people who can afford your coffee live; say, people who make more than $45,000 a year. You can find these areas by writing an expression, called a query, that instructs ArcExplorer to find those areas where the query expression is true.

**3**   Click the Query Builder button. The Query Builder dialog box displays.

The dialog box contains a list of field names (at the left), that is, all the different kinds of demographic data that were collected for this theme; a set of operators (center) that will do the actual work of narrowing down the data; and a list of sample values (right). When you click on a field name, all the unique values for that field display in the Sample Values list.

To build a query, you click on a field name, click on an operator, then click on a value or type it in. As you build the query, it displays in the query text box in the center of the dialog box. (You can also type your query directly in the query text box, but your typing has to be very accurate, or the Query Builder won't perform the query.)

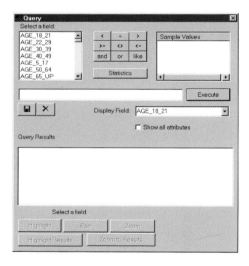

**4**   In the Query Builder dialog box, scroll down through the list of field names. If necessary, you can check the file *CensusFieldDefinitions.htm* in the *Explore* directory of the CD for a translation of some of the more obscure abbreviations.

Click on *PCI00*. You see the values for this field display in the Sample Values list.

**5** Click the greater-than operator (>). It displays in the query text box.

**6** Type in the value **45000** at the end of the expression in the query text box. Your expression should look like this: **PCI00 > 45000**

In English, this means, "Find all the areas in which per capita annual income is more than $45,000."

**7** Choose *PCI00* as the Display Field. This will display the values for this field for all the matching records.

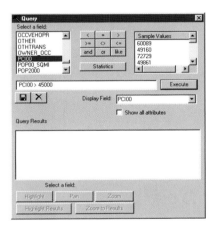

**8** Click the Execute button. ArcExplorer searches the attribute table for all the records that match your request. Matches for areas having a per capita income greater than $45,000 are shown in the query results section of the dialog.

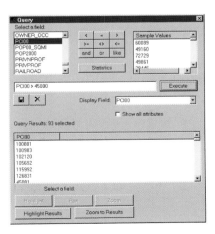

**9** Click the Highlight Results button. All of the matching areas are high-lighted in your map view in bright yellow. Move the dialog window to the side so you can see your map view.

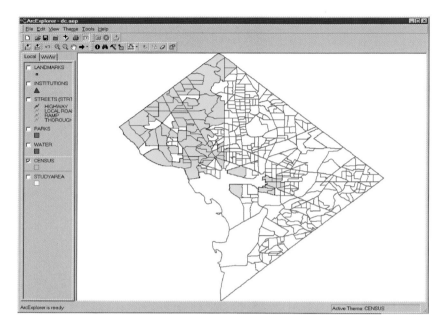

Now you need to find areas where there's a strong need for coffee; say, people with long commutes to work. You need to build an expression that finds the areas where people make more than $45,000 a year and have long commutes.

**10** Clear the old expression by clicking the Delete button. Build the following expression in the dialog: **PCI00 > 45000 and AVGTRVLWRK > 30**

In English, this means, "Find all the areas where people make more than $45,000 a year and, in the same area, travel more than thirty minutes to get to work."

**11** Choose *PCI00* as the Display Field.

**12**   Click the Execute button. The records that match your query are shown in the query results section.

**13**   Click the Highlight Results button. All of the matching areas are high-lighted in your map view in bright yellow.

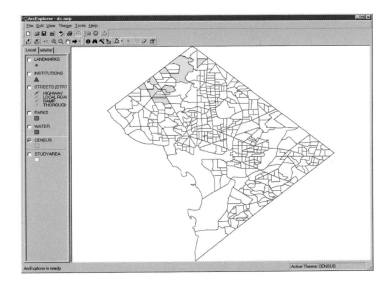

Try some other queries. Remember, a translation of the census abbreviations is contained on the CD.

**14**   When you're finished, close the Map Query dialog box by clicking on the X in its upper right corner.

Chapter 3                                    Exploration 3-5   Where is it? (part two)

Finding answers with digital maps

# Exploration 3-5   Where is it? (part two)

Another way to find things is to use the Address Matcher tool. This tool allows you to find the location of a particular address, a process known as address matching. It's the computer equivalent of pushing pins into a wall map to show the location of an address. Address matching in ArcExplorer is best used to compare the location of an address with the location of other geographic features, such as parks, flood zones, or shopping centers.

Suppose you're headed to Washington, D.C., for business, but have a little free time to see some sights. You have the choice of staying at one of three hotels. You want to see where each is so you can choose the one closest to the major tourist attractions.

First, you need to tell ArcExplorer which theme contains the streets and specify the special attributes that allow address matching to work. Next, you specify an address to look for. ArcExplorer then places a label to show the location of the address on your map.

**1** Make the STUDYAREA theme active and click the Zoom to Active Theme button.

**2** Turn on all the themes except INSTITUTIONS.

**3** Make the STREETS theme active.

**4** From the Theme menu, choose Address Matcher Properties. The Address Matcher Properties dialog box displays. The required input fields have field names from the STREETS theme filled in. These field names correspond to the default names required by ArcExplorer.

Exploration 3-5   Where is it? (part two)

*Chapter 3*

Finding answers with digital maps

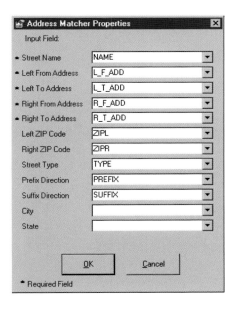

We won't go into an explanation of these fields at this point. If you're inter-ested in learning more about how address matching works, consult the Address Matching topic in ArcExplorer Help.

**5** Click OK to make the theme matchable. Once the Address Matcher prop-erties are set, they needn't be set again during your current ArcExplorer session. Click OK again when you see that the address-matching index has been built.

Now you can find the location of each hotel address using a street number and name. The three hotel addresses you want to find are:

*Holiday Inn Central, 501 Rhode Island Avenue*

*Capital Hilton, 1001 16th Street*

*Jurys Normandy Inn Hotel, 2118 Wyoming Ave., NW*

Chapter 3

Exploration 3-5   Where is it? (part two)

Finding answers with digital maps

First you'll find the location of the Holiday Inn and see how close it is to the landmarks.

6   Click the Address Matcher button.

7   In the Address Matching dialog box, choose *Address* under Options and enter **501 Rhode Island Avenue** as the address you want to match.

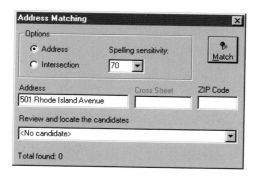

8   Click the Match button. ArcExplorer finds the address and puts a label on the map. The map view pans and zooms to the location of the Holiday Inn. Move the dialog window to the side so you can see your map view. This hotel is near some landmarks, but perhaps you could be even closer.

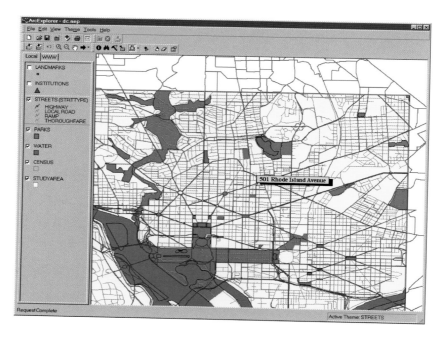

Exploration 3-5    Where is it? (part two)

*Chapter 3*

Finding answers with digital maps

Now find the location of the Capital Hilton.

**9**    In the Address Matching dialog box, enter **1001 16th Street** as the address you want to match.

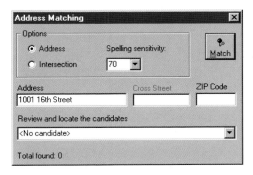

**10**    Click the Match button. The map view pans and zooms to the location of the Capital Hilton. This hotel offers a very central location in relation to the landmarks. You'll probably stay here, but you'll find the last hotel location just in case.

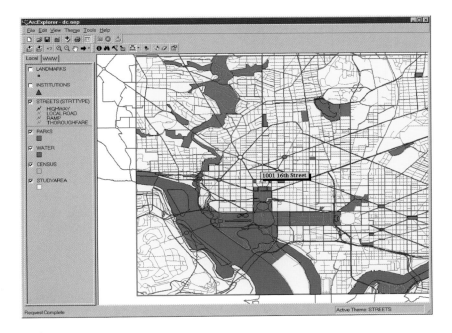

Chapter 3

Exploration 3-5   Where is it? (part two)

Finding answers with digital maps

Find the location of the Jurys Normandy Inn Hotel.

**11** In the Address Matching dialog box, enter **2118 Wyoming Ave., NW** as the address you want to match.

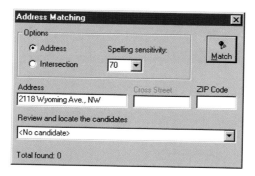

**12** Click the Match button. The map view pans and zooms to the location of the Jurys Normandy Inn Hotel. Like the Holiday Inn, this hotel is too far away. You'll stay at the Capital Hilton.

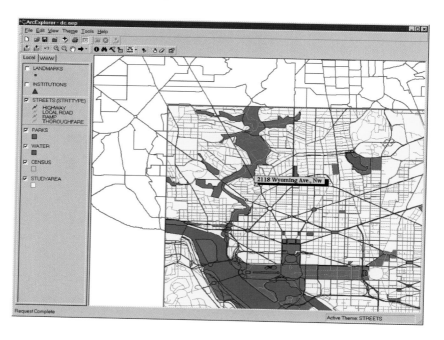

Exploration 3-5   Where is it? (part two)                                    *Chapter 3*

Finding answers with digital maps

**13**   Click the Clear Selection button when you're finished viewing the location.

**14**   Close the project without saving any changes.

Address matching is one of the most common operations people perform with a GIS. In fact, addresses are probably the most commonly used form of geographic data. You'll find many uses for address matching. You could locate the address of a new restaurant that got rave reviews in the paper. You could find the location of your house in relation to flood zones. You might want to see the location of a house for sale listed in the newspaper, and see whether it's farther away from the flood zones. On a map you create for your friends, you could pinpoint the location of the party you're having to celebrate buying the new, flood-free house.

# CHAPTER 4

# Telling stories with digital maps

IMAGINE YOU'RE LOST, in a city far away from home—perhaps Venice. You need to find the nearest vaporetto (water bus) stop, so that you can get to the Santa Lucia train station and begin the journey home. But you're hopelessly lost, somewhere near the Rialto, you think, and time is running out. Every corner you turn brings you deeper into the serpentine depths of the famous city, nowhere near the Grand Canal where the vaporettos travel. You speak no Italian, and no Italian seems to speak any English. In desperation you pull out your paper map of Venice—it looks like a plate of capellini splattered onto the page—and show it to a kindly-looking shop owner. He speaks no English either, but he traces out the route to the nearest vaporetto stop on the map, using a blunt pencil. Thanks to the map, you make your train on time.

A map at its core is one of the best tools ever devised for communicating with other people: get lost in a strange city and a map will get you found.

Now that you've seen the wealth of information contained in digital maps—GIS—the next step is to create your own. GIS maps have several advantages over paper maps. You can customize them for any use and then print them out. Or, when the geography of an area changes, you can update the GIS to reflect the new reality. And, unlike a paper map, you can e-mail a GIS map.

The appearance of a map makes a big difference in how well it communicates information. Each dot, line, or area on a map represents something in the real world—a city, a road, a country. You can draw these features any way you want, although as you probably already know, there are some traditions in map symbology: a double red line often indicates a major highway, a tent is a recreation area, a tiny plane is an airport. Even colors are traditional: green means vegetation, blue means water. Such symbols need to be consistent throughout the map.

In this chapter, you will learn different ways to create GIS maps using ArcExplorer's cartographic tools.

# Exploration 4-1   A trip to Rio de Janeiro

Like Venice, Rio de Janeiro has welcomed millions of tourists year in and year out, most of them getting lost at one point or another, and thus in need of maps. This exercise will show you how easy it is to put together a basic yet informative map of the area of Rio de Janeiro called Ipanema—a town made famous in the late 1950s in a hit song by Brazilian songwriter Antonio Carlos Jobim.

**ArcExplorer**

1   Start ArcExplorer, if necessary.

**2** Click the Open Project button. Navigate to the *explore\rio* directory on the CD, choose the project file *rio.AEP,* and then click Open.

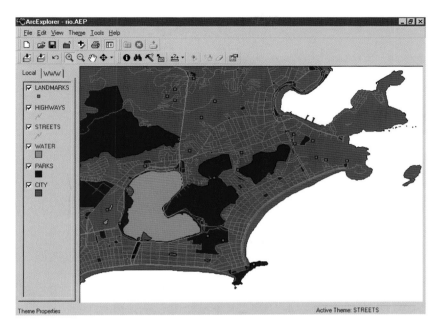

The map view contains themes of streets, highways, parks, landmarks, and water. However, the colors aren't very interesting, and it's hard to distinguish one theme from another. ArcExplorer assigns colors at random, so it's up to you to pick some that are more interesting.

First you'll change the CITY theme to light yellow so features in other themes will stand out.

**3** Make the CITY theme active in the legend.

**4**   To display the Theme Properties dialog box, click the Theme Properties button or double-click on the theme name, CITY, in the legend.

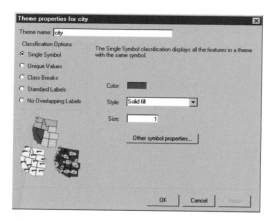

In the Theme Properties dialog box, the theme name box shows you which theme you're working with. Classification Options shows you the way in which the features of this theme are displayed. In this case, the classification option is *Single Symbol*, which means that all the features in the theme are currently symbolized as shown in the dialog.

**5**   Click the Color box to display the Color dialog box. Choose *light yellow* and click OK.

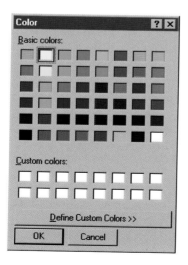

**6** Click OK in the Theme Properties dialog box to apply your change.

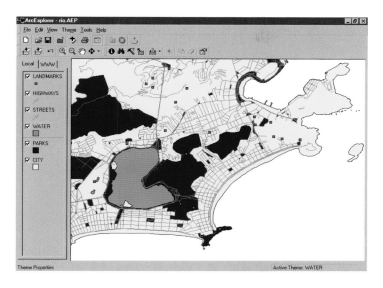

Do the same for the WATER theme.

**7** Make the WATER theme active and use Theme Properties to make water *blue.*

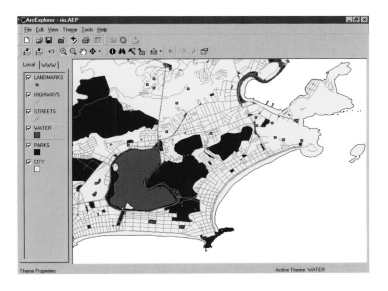

Now that water looks right, make parks green.

**8** Make the PARKS theme active and use Theme Properties to make parks *green.*

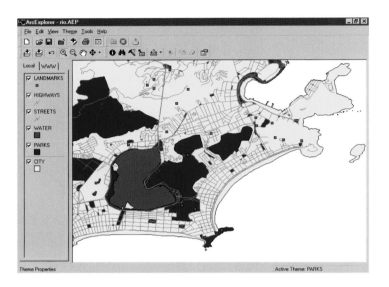

Now you'll select an appropriate symbol for streets.

**9** Make the STREETS theme active and click the Theme Properties button.

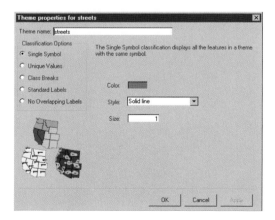

**10** In the Theme Properties dialog box, click the Color box to display the Color dialog box. Choose *dark gray* and click OK.

Notice that the size property of the line is 1 (the default value). The size property controls the thickness of the lines on your map. The larger the value, the thicker the line. Keep a value of 1 for the STREETS theme.

**11** Click OK in the Theme Properties dialog box to apply your change.

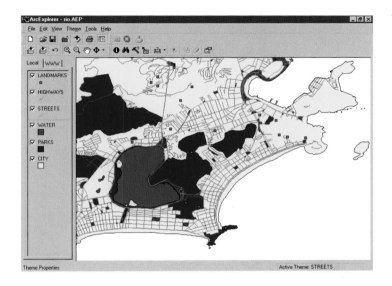

**12** Make the HIGHWAYS theme active and use Theme Properties to make highways *red*. Since highways are usually bigger and used by more people than are streets, specify a size of *2*.

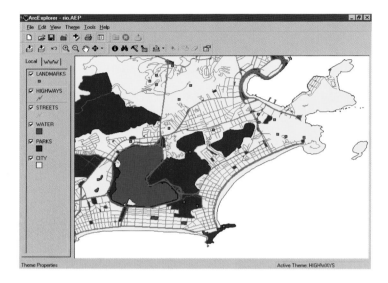

Now you'll change the landmarks symbol.

  **13** Make the LANDMARKS theme active, and use Theme Properties to make landmarks *red*. Use the Style pull-down menu to choose *Triangle marker*. Specify a size of *6*.

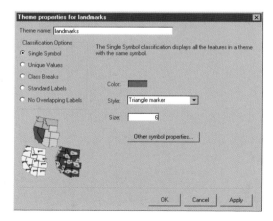

**14** Click OK in the Theme Properties dialog box to make the changes.

Now zoom in on Ipanema, the most famous neighborhood of Rio de Janeiro.

 **15** Click the Zoom In tool and create a box as shown in the following graphic.

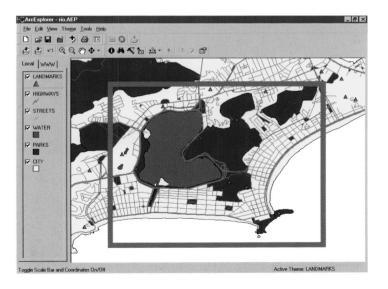

Now you'll create labels for each of the landmarks on your map. You can do this in the Theme Properties dialog box also, using the Standard Labels and No Overlapping Labels buttons. The buttons create labels using a specified text font that you get from a field in the table.

Use Standard Labels to place the labels according to choices you set.

Use No Overlapping Labels to keep labels from crowding or overlapping. This is good for labeling features such as streets. You can also use this option to create a colored background under the label so the text is easily readable.

**16** Click the Theme Properties button to display the Theme Properties dialog box.

**17** Choose *No Overlapping Labels* under Classification Options.

Choose *NAME* as the text field.

In the label placement options, choose *Place on.*

Click on the *Mask labels* option.

Click in the *Mask color* box and choose *white.*

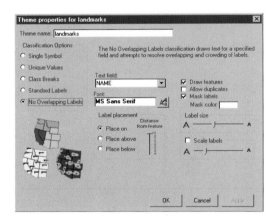

Click Apply to check the labels. They may appear too large on the map. If so, adjust the label size slider and then click Apply to check the size. Repeat this procedure until your labels are big enough to be legible, but not so big that they crowd each other out.

Click OK in the Theme Properties dialog box when you're finished.

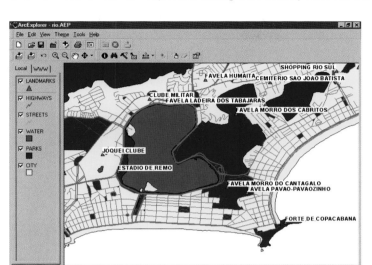

Since the white area in this map view is actually water, set the background of the map to blue.

**18**   Select Map Display Properties from the View menu. The Map Display Properties dialog box displays.

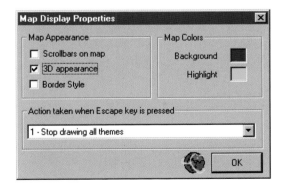

**19**   Under Map Colors, click *Background* to display the Color dialog box. Choose *blue,* then click OK to close the dialog box.

**20** Click OK to close the Map Display Properties dialog box.

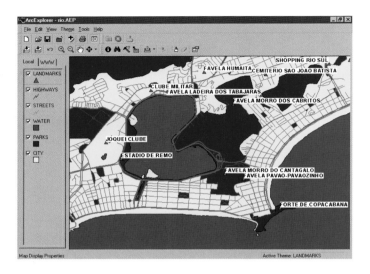

Now add a scale bar so that the distances are in context.

**21** Choose Display Scale Bar from the View menu. A scale bar appears below the map view.

**22** Right-click the scale bar and set the map units to *Decimal Degrees.* Set the scale units to *Miles* and the screen units to *Inches.*

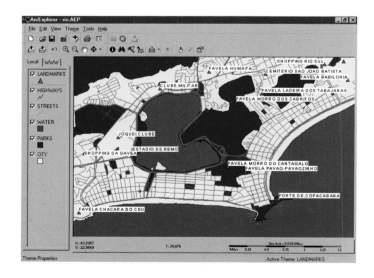

Your map is now ready to print.

**23** Click the Print tool. The Print Map dialog box displays. This is where you choose a printer and where you give your map a title.

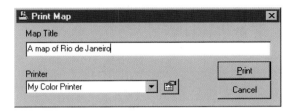

**24** In the Print Map dialog box, enter **A map of Rio de Janeiro** as the title of your map.

**25** Click Print.

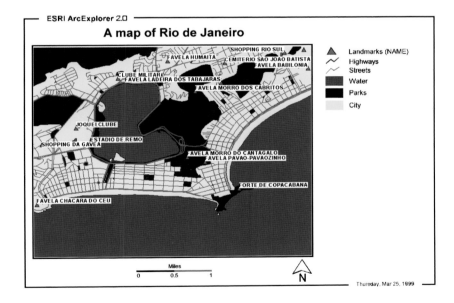

Your finished map will appear as shown here, formatted with north arrow, scale bar, legend, and title.

**26** Close the project without saving any changes.

# Exploration 4-2   **Symbolize a map of Prague**

In the previous exploration, you symbolized all the features in a theme with the same symbol, but you can also use symbols that reveal more information about a feature. The decisions here aren't as simple as assigning green to parks and red lines to highways. For example, a theme of roads may have an attribute that describes the type of road—two-lane highway, four-lane highway, major street, and minor street. You can use this attribute to assign different symbols to each type so your audience can easily tell them apart.

Suppose you work for a university that offers its students a chance to attend summer school in the historic city of Prague in the Czech Republic. During the summer, students attend class Monday through Thursday and have the remaining three days to enjoy the sights and atmosphere of the city. To help recruit students, you want to create a map showing the historic center of Prague, its major tourist attractions, and restaurants. Then you want to save the map as an image that you can put on your university's Web page and in a printed student newsletter.

**1** Start ArcExplorer, if necessary.

**2** Click the Open Project button. Navigate to the *explore\prague* directory on the CD, choose the project file *prague.AEP,* and then click Open.

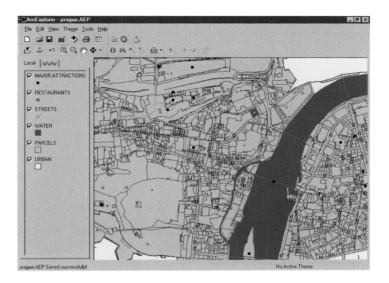

When the project opens, you see the historic area of Prague. Themes include parcels, streets, restaurants, major attractions, and water. Although each theme uses a single symbol to represent its features, each feature contains several different attributes. For example, the RESTAURANTS theme contains an attribute to identify whether each symbol represents a pub, a coffeehouse, or a full-serve, sit-down restaurant.

**3** Make the PARCELS theme active. Use the Identify tool to click on some of the areas.

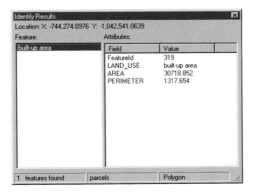

Notice that each area you click on has a land-use attribute that specifies whether that piece of land is parkland, built-up area, pavement, or some other type. You may need to zoom in to distinguish one parcel from another.

**4**   Dismiss the Identify Results dialog box by clicking the X in its corner.

You'll assign different colors to each type of land use.

**5**   Click the Theme Properties button to display the Theme Properties dialog box.

**6**   To apply a different color to each unique land use, choose *Unique Values* under the Classification Options heading.

Choose *LAND_USE* as the field in the Field pull-down menu.

These default colors are probably not all appropriate for the features they represent, since the software assigns them at random. You'll choose some new ones.

In the Theme Properties dialog box, click on the color to the left of the words *built-up area.* The Symbol Properties dialog box displays. Choose *light red* as the color. Click OK.

Repeat this procedure for the remaining colors, clicking on each in turn and changing its color. You may not have to change all of them.

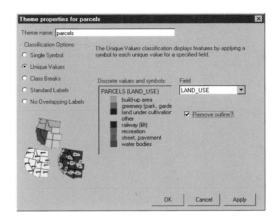

For *greenery*, assign *light green*.

For *land under cultivation*, assign *green*.

For *other*, assign *light gray*.

For *railway*, assign *purple*.

For *recreation*, assign *red*.

For *street, pavement*, assign *dark gray*.

For *water bodies*, assign *blue*.

When you're finished symbolizing land uses, check the *Remove outline?* box and then click OK in the Theme Properties dialog box.

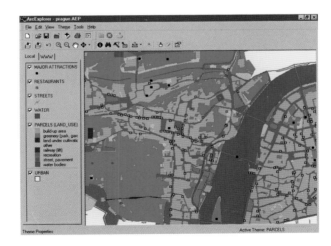

Readers of your map can now easily distinguish the different types of land use.

Now look at the attributes for the restaurants.

**7**  Make the RESTAURANTS theme active. Use the Identify tool to click on several of the points.

Each restaurant has a name and a type.

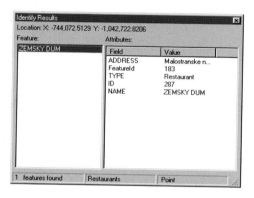

Next, you'll symbolize the restaurants with different point symbols so students can tell whether each is a sit-down establishment, a pub, or a coffee-house. The procedure is much the same as the one you just followed for land uses.

**8**  After dismissing the Identify Results dialog box, make the RESTAURANTS theme active in the legend.

**9**  Click the Theme Properties button to display the Theme Properties dialog box.

Choose *Unique Values* under Classification Options.

Choose *TYPE* as the field in the Field pull-down menu.

You'll now choose different symbols for each type of restaurant.

In the Theme Properties dialog box, click on the symbol to the left of the words *Cafe, Coffeehouse*. The Symbol Properties dialog box displays.

Choose *orange* as the color, *Circle marker* as the style, and *6* as the size.

Telling stories with digital maps

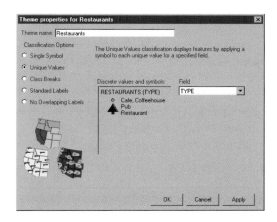

Repeat for the remaining symbols, clicking on each symbol in turn and modifying the symbol properties for each.

For Pub, choose *dark blue* as the color, *Triangle marker* as the style, and *6* as the size.

For Restaurant, choose *dark green* as the color, *Square marker* as the style, and *6* as the size.

When you finish symbolizing the restaurants, click OK in the Theme Properties dialog box.

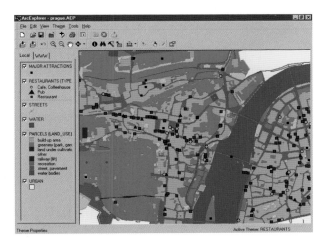

Now that the different types of restaurants can be distinguished, symbolize and label the major attractions.

**10** Make the MAJOR ATTRACTIONS theme active and use Theme Properties to make the attractions *yellow.* Use the Style pull-down menu to choose *Triangle marker.* Specify *6* as the size.

Choose *No Overlapping Labels* under Classification Options.

Choose *NAME* as the text field.

Click on the *Mask labels* option.

Click in the *Mask color* box and choose *white.*

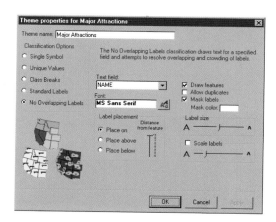

Click Apply in the Theme Properties dialog box to view the labels in your map view. Adjust the label size with the label size slider if they appear too large. Click OK when you're satisfied with the label size.

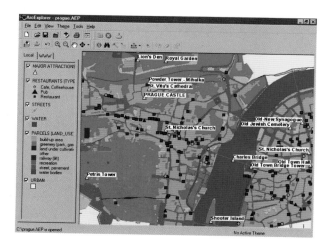

Your map is now well symbolized and labeled. (Note that there really are two churches named after St. Nicholas in Prague.) All that's left to do is save your map so others can use it.

From the Edit menu, there are several options for saving your map view. Choose Copy to Clipboard if you plan to paste it into another Windows program. Choose Copy to File if you want to create a file to use anytime.

Choose BMP (Windows bitmap) if your map view contains a scanned map or aerial photograph. Otherwise, choose EMF (enhanced metafile).

**11**  From the Edit menu, choose Copy to File (EMF). ArcExplorer prompts you to specify a name and a location for the new file. You might save the file in the directory *C:\prague* as *prague.emf*.

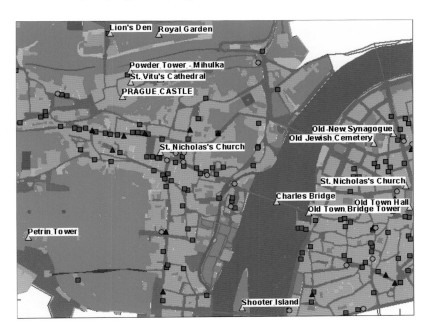

Now you can use the file in another Windows application such as Microsoft Word or in a drawing program like Adobe® Illustrator®. Your drawing program may allow you to convert the file to GIF or JPG format for use on your personal Web page.

**12** Close the project without saving any changes.

You now have an informative map of Prague that gives students a good idea not only of the city's geography, but also its history and its recreational possibilities. You can put the map on the school's Web page, or include it in a newsletter mailed to students.

# Exploration 4-3 Create a demographic map of New York City

Most of the data that you have been adding to your digital maps up to now has been the kind that people are used to seeing on maps—that is, information that describes the location and attributes of physical objects, such as streets or railroads or visual landmarks.

But physical objects are only a small part of the information available for mapping in a GIS. The power of GIS, as has been noted, lies in its ability to map any kind of information, as long as it has a geographic component; you are limited only by your imagination.

Information about people has become a powerful new data source in the GIS world, especially for those in industry and government. Mapping the characteristics of a specific population—also known as demographics—and its consumer, political, and entertainment preferences has become big business, for reasons not difficult to understand.

But geographic information about people is not exclusively reserved for big business and big government, nor should it be. Readers of this book can also take such information and answer questions about who Americans are and what they want. Using freely available data from the U.S. Census Bureau Internet sites, anyone with GIS software such as ArcExplorer can create a human map of the world they live in.

Such maps can be invaluable for a variety of purposes at the local and neighborhood level. Community organizers could map where their activism might be needed most. Parent–school groups could track the need for recreation programs, or the effectiveness of educational ones. And small businesses could see at a glance the location of potentially lucrative new markets.

In fact, businesses of all sizes use GIS for just this purpose, which makes it ideal for the next ArcExplorer exercise. In it, you'll see where different kinds of people live in New York City, in order to decide where would be the best place to target a new marketing campaign for your company.

First, you'll need to copy the data from the ArcExplorer CD to your own hard drive.

1  Create a folder on your PC to store the data. For example, you might create a folder named *gis_data* on your C: drive.

2  Copy the *newyork* folder from the *explore* folder on the CD to the location you just created.

Now that the data is on your PC, you're ready to create your maps.

3  Start ArcExplorer, if necessary.

**ArcExplorer**

4  Click the Open Project button. Navigate to the *newyork* folder you copied, choose the project file *newyork.AEP,* and then click Open. The project opens, and you see a map view of some residential areas of Manhattan. It contains several themes, including WATER, PLACES, and CENSUS.

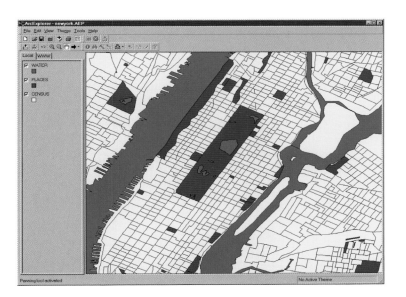

**5** Make the CENSUS theme active and click the Identify button. Using your mouse, click around in several different areas to learn about them. The CENSUS theme contains the same kind of demographic information about Manhattan that you saw in the Washington, D.C., exploration.

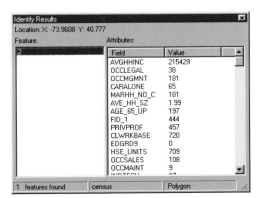

**6** Close the Identify Results dialog box.

Now you'll create a couple of maps so you can see how some of these attributes are distributed throughout Manhattan. Specifically, you'll be looking for areas that have a high proportion of high-income wage earners, and areas that have a high proportion of college graduates. The areas where these groups intersect will be your target marketing areas.

First, you'll create a map of median income.

**7**  Click the Theme Properties button to display the Theme Properties dialog box.

Choose *Class Breaks* under Classification Options.

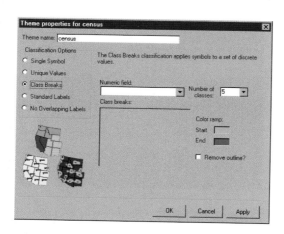

The Class Breaks option is used to create a graduated color map, such as this one, from numeric data. Similar numeric values are grouped together as ranges, or classes. A different color is applied to each range.

**8**  In the *Numeric field* pull-down menu, scroll down and choose the field *MEDHHINC*.

**9**  In the *Number of classes* pull-down menu, choose *7*.

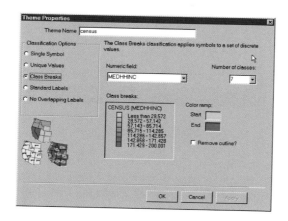

Seven is a good number because most people can visually distinguish about that many classes, give or take a couple. Depending on the quality of your monitor or printer, however, five classes may be a more practical limit for you.

Now you'll create a color ramp to represent the median income. A color ramp uses colors to indicate rank or order among classes. The colors progress from light to dark. With numeric data, lower values should use lighter colors and higher values should use darker colors. Different shades of the same or related colors work well; a progression of light red, red, and dark red is easier to interpret than green, blue, and red.

**10** Click the Start color box to select a starting color for your color ramp. The Color dialog box will display.

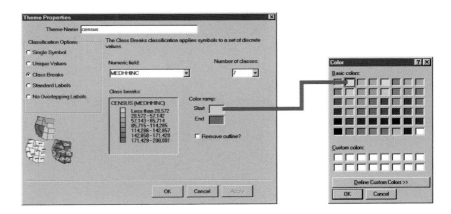

Select a shade of light yellow and then click OK.

**11** Click the End color box to select the ending color for your color ramp. This time, select a shade of dark red and then click OK.

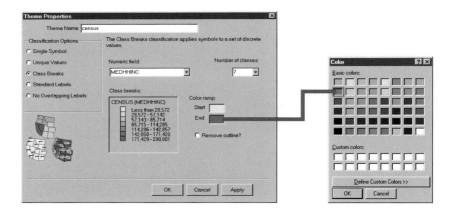

**12** Click OK in the Theme Properties dialog box to make the map.

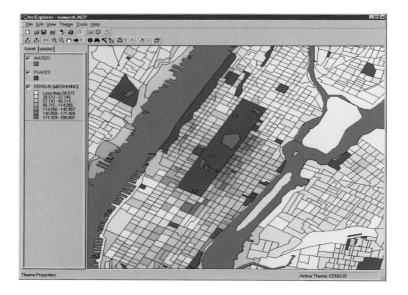

Your map shows lower income with lighter colors and higher income with darker colors. As you might expect, the higher-income groups tend to be clustered around Central Park. In fact, some very wealthy folks live in this area.

You can easily change the subject of the map by selecting a different demographic field—for example, the areas that have a high number of college graduates.

**13** Click the Theme Properties button to display the Theme Properties dialog box. In the *Numeric field* pull-down menu, scroll down and choose the field *EDBACHDEG*.

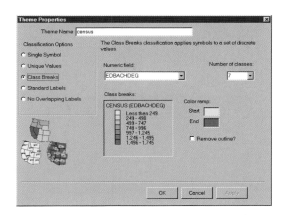

**14** Click OK in the Theme Properties dialog box.

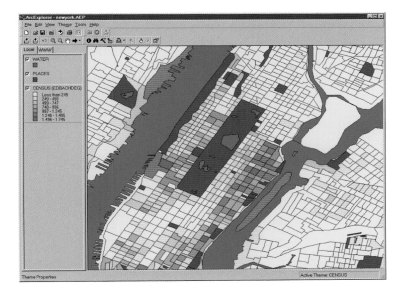

The subject of your map changes to show the distribution of people who graduated from college. Perhaps not surprisingly, it has the same general appearance as the previous map. You now have a pretty good idea of where your marketing campaign will be directed.

You'll save this map as an ArcExplorer project. That way, not only will you be able to view the map quickly at a later time, but you can also distribute your map digitally for others to see.

**15** Choose Save As from the File menu. Specify a file name of *default.aep*. Save the project in the *newyork* folder you created earlier. Click Save. The project is saved to your local hard disk. (See the ArcExplorer Help topic "Zip archives" for important information on projects named *default*.)

 **16** Click the Theme Properties button to display the Theme Properties dialog box. Specify some different attributes in the *Numeric field* pull-down menu. You might also wish to experiment with different colors in the color ramp.

When you're done looking at other attributes, open the project you saved to display your college graduate map.

 **17** Click the Open Project button. You'll be asked if you want to save changes to your project.

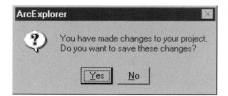

Click No. The Open ArcExplorer Project dialog box displays.

Click on the project *default.aep*. Click Open.

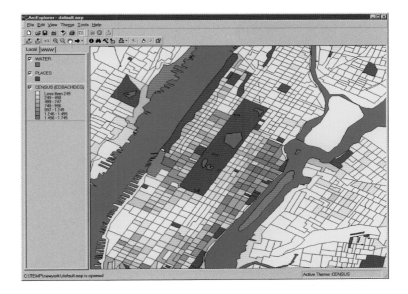

The map of college graduates in Manhattan once again displays on your screen. You can e-mail an image of the map to your colleagues as a file attachment, and begin to plan your company's marketing campaign.

**18**  Close the project without saving any changes.

### SHARE A PROJECT

ArcExplorer projects that you create contain paths to folders that reside on your computer, such as *C:\gis_data\newyork*. Before you can share your ArcExplorer project with others, you must edit the project file so that all paths are relative. That way, the projects will open on all computers, regardless of the path where the data resides. See the ArcExplorer Help topic "Creating relative pathnames" to learn how to edit project files so they work on other computers.

# CHAPTER 5

# Building the digital map

Up to this chapter, you've been living a pretty sheltered life. We've provided you the appropriate data files for cities such as San Diego and Prague so you can get accustomed to working with a GIS without worrying about other issues. But the reality is that geographic data in the actual world comes in many different formats. This chapter introduces you to some of them, and then helps you put these diverse formats together to make an even more powerful map.

# Varieties of geographic data

Geographic data is information about the earth's surface and the objects found on it. This information comes in three basic forms: map data, attribute data, and image data.

Map data contains the location and shape of geographic features. To represent real-world objects, maps use three basic shapes: points, lines, and areas (in a GIS, these are commonly referred to as points, lines, and polygons). Any object can be represented using one of these shapes.

Points represent objects that have discrete locations and are too small to be depicted as areas, such as schools, churches, train stations, and firehouses. Lines represent objects that have length but are too narrow to be depicted as polygons, such as freeways, roads, railroads, bridges, and creeks. Areas represent objects too large to be depicted as points or lines, such as large rivers, parks, lakes, golf courses, and forests.

## Map Data

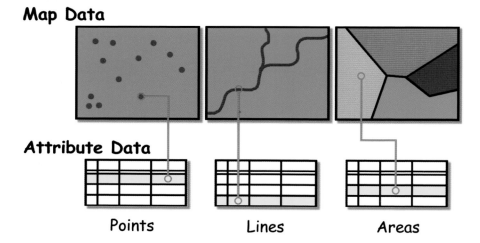

## Attribute Data

Points          Lines          Areas

Attribute data is the descriptive data that GIS links to map features. Attribute data is collected and compiled for specific areas like states, census tracts, cities, and so on, and often comes packaged with map data.

Image data includes such diverse elements as satellite images, aerial photographs, and scanned data (data that's been converted from printed to digital format).

Geographic data comes in many different formats.

# Varieties of geographic data files

The format of the data you choose must be compatible with your GIS and the data you already have. While formats can be a complex subject, at this point in your GIS career there are only a few that you need to know to begin creating good maps.

**Shapefiles**

One of the most common formats you're likely to encounter, and the easiest to use, is the shapefile. A shapefile can represent a point feature such as a city, a line feature such as a highway, or an area feature such as a county. Shapefiles store the geometric location and attribute information of these features.

Shapefiles are actually made up of at least three underlying files that must be kept together in the same folder or directory. Most of the time they're invisible to you and you don't have to worry about them. If you have to, you can identify them by their extensions (the suffix on the end of a file name): .shp, .shx, .dbf. You're most likely to encounter these file types when you unzip a compressed file.

One reason for knowing about these three is that you can use them as an alternative way to add a theme to an ArcExplorer map view. Although most of the time you'll add a theme by using the Add Theme button, the alternative method is to drag any of the three file types listed (SHP, SHX, DBF) from a Windows folder directly into the map view.

**Geodatabase**

Used within or as part of a relational database, the geodatabase acts as a container for various kinds of spatial and attribute data, and for all the complex relationships that can exist among those pieces of data. With a geodatabase, you can create a complex GIS data model that represents spatial relationships in the real world. Geodatabases can only be used with more advanced software such as ArcGIS™.

**ArcInfo coverages**

Another common format you'll likely run into is called an ArcInfo™ coverage.

ArcInfo is another kind of GIS software from ESRI. Like shapefiles, coverages also store geographic features such as points, lines, and areas, along with their attributes. Some ArcInfo coverages can contain more than one type of feature. For example, a coverage containing area features such as land parcels may also contain line features that store information about the boundaries between the parcels.

89

Since a theme in ArcExplorer can only represent one class of features from an ArcInfo coverage, you choose which class you want the theme to represent. However, you can add several themes to a view from the same ArcInfo coverage, each based on a different class.

*ArcInfo interchange files*

Often, ArcInfo coverages are contained within files with a .e00 extension. These have to be converted to coverages using a special utility program called IMPORT71, which is included in the *Software\Import71* folder on the companion CD. Instructions for installing and using IMPORT71 are found in the file *Readme.htm* in this folder.

**Images**

Images are intrinsically interesting. It would probably take about a thousand words to explain why. Instead, we'll just describe the two types of images you're most likely to run across, aerial (or satellite) photos and scanned images.

*Aerial photographs*

Aerial photographs make compelling backgrounds for your other GIS data. You can display the location of flood zones on an image of your hometown, or simply show a bird's-eye view of your neighborhood.

On the Internet, you're most likely to find aerial photographs in a format called digital orthophoto quads, or DOQ. Most are free. There are also many private vendors that sell aerial photos and satellite imagery.

*A DOQ image of Boston, Massachusetts, obtained for free via the Internet.*

**Scanned maps**     Scanned maps, like aerial photos, can be used in the background with your other geographic data.

The most common scanned maps you'll find are topographic maps. Topographic maps represent a three-dimensional surface on a flat piece of paper. These are the types of maps commonly used for outdoor recreation—for planning hikes and camping trips—as well as for urban planning, resource development, and surveying. The map of San Diego you first looked at in chapter 2 is a scanned topographic map.

A free source of digital topographic maps for the United States is the digital raster graphic (DRG), scanned from a U.S. Geological Survey standard-series topographic map. DRGs are increasingly being made available over the Internet. They are useful for exploring the terrain where you plan to go hiking or mountain biking,  or for any other purpose where you need to know the elevation of the earth.

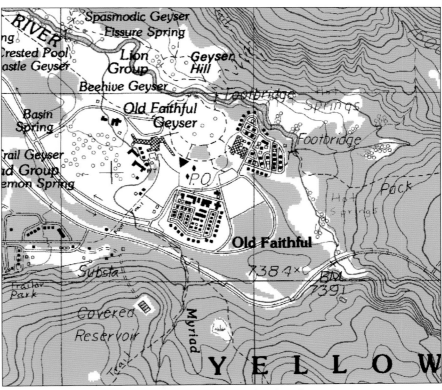

*A DRG image showing part of Yellowstone National Park.*

Other sources of high-quality but inexpensive scanned topographic maps include Sure!MAPS RASTER from Titan Systems Corporation, and TOPO! from the National Geographic Society. Both offer complete coverage of the United States. You can find, preview, and obtain these maps on Geography Network, which you'll learn about in chapter 6.

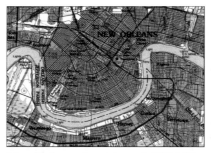

*New Orleans, Louisiana, 1:100,000 scale. Copyright © Titan Systems Corporation.*

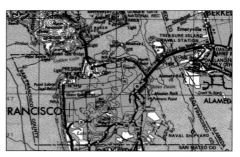

*San Francisco, California, 1:250,000 scale. Copyright © Titan Systems Corporation.*

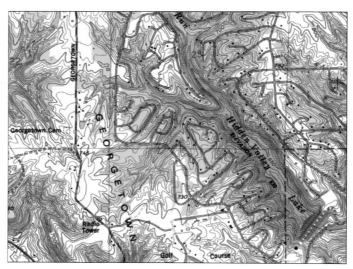

*An area near Lawrenceburg, Indiana, 1:24,000 scale. Copyright © Titan Systems Corporation.*

**Image formats**  Images come in a variety of formats with their own extensions. You don't have to worry about how they work, but it is helpful to be aware of the different types so you can recognize them. The most common formats you're likely to encounter include TIFF (*.tif), MrSID® (*.sid), JPEG (*.jpg), Bitmap (*.bmp), and IMAGINE (*.img). ArcExplorer can read all of these and several others. See the ArcExplorer help for a complete list.

# Exploration 5-1   **Putting it all together**

Photo courtesy of Abhijit Jas

Now that you understand the diversity of geographic data formats, it's time to try putting them all into one smooth-looking, easy-to-understand GIS map, in much the same way that GIS professionals do. In this exercise, you will assemble a variety of data sets into a map of the capital city of Texas, Austin. To make the exercise more realistic, assume that you are moving your family to Austin. In such a scenario, you'd be mostly interested in certain kinds of geographic information, those that would help you make decisions about the best places in the Austin area to look for a house to live in. You'd probably want to know where schools are located, and where the major streets and landmarks are located; perhaps you'd also like some environmental information, so that you don't wind up moving to an area prone to flooding, or other such problem. After all, it's as true in GIS as it is in any other field—the more information you have, the better decision you can make.

**1** Start ArcExplorer, if necessary.

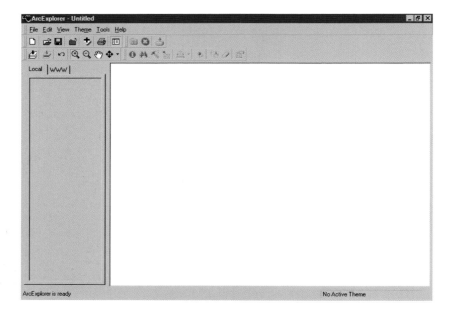

You see a blank map view and a blank legend.

**2** Click the Add Theme button. The Add Theme(s) dialog box displays.

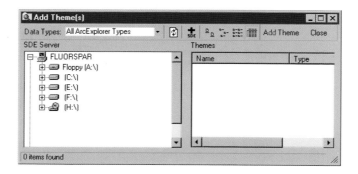

In this box are two windows. On the left is a list of all the drives and directories on your computer. This is where you find your data.

**3** On the left side of the dialog box, find your CD drive. Then go to the *explore\austin* directory on the CD.

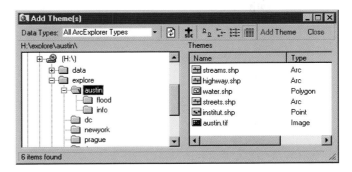

When you open the *austin* folder, you'll see several different themes, in different formats, listed in the window at the right. At the top of the box, in the Data Types window, *All ArcExplorer Types* is the default choice. This means the right window will show shapefiles, coverages, or image files. If you have a lot of different data types available, you can use the Data Types pull-down menu to limit the kinds of file formats that will be listed in the window.

Since aerial photographs work well as backgrounds, you'll look to see what images are available.

**4** Using the Data Types pull-down menu, choose *Supported Images*.

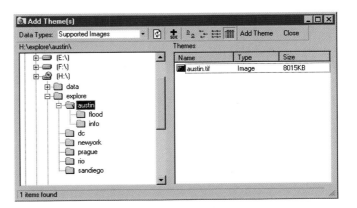

You see that only one image, *austin.tif*, is listed in the themes list. You'll add that image to the map view.

**5**   Click on the name of the file *austin.tif*. Click Add Theme, then click Close.

The theme is added to the legend as AUSTIN (Image).

**6**   Turn on the theme AUSTIN in the legend.

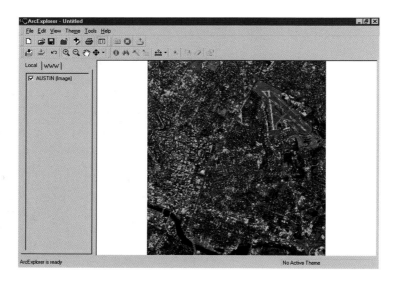

Now you'll add your shapefiles to the map view.

**7**   Click the Add Theme button. In the Add Theme(s) dialog box, choose *Shapefiles* as the data type.

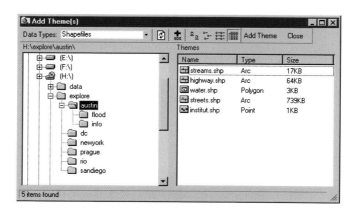

Only shapefiles appear in the Themes list.

**8**  Click on water.shp and Add Theme,
streams.shp and Add Theme,
streets.shp and Add Theme,
highway.shp and Add Theme,
institut.shp and Add Theme.

**9**  Turn on the five new themes in the legend.

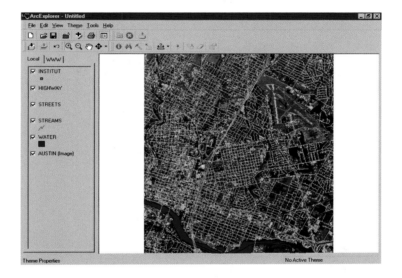

Since ArcExplorer assigns random colors to the new themes, you may need to assign more appropriate ones.

**10** Use Theme Properties in turn for each theme to assign appropriate colors and symbols (you learned how to do this in chapter 4). Following are some suggestions:

WATER: *blue*

STREAMS: *blue*

STREETS: *light gray* with a size of *1*

HIGHWAYS: *red* with a size of *2*

INSTITUT: Use a unique value classification and choose *TYPE* as the field. For each type, assign symbols as follows: for Cemetery, use *green* as the color, *Triangle marker* as the style, and *7* as the size; for School, use *yellow* as the color, *Circle marker* as the style, and *7* as the size; for Hospital, use *red* as the color, *Square marker* as the style, and *7* as the size.

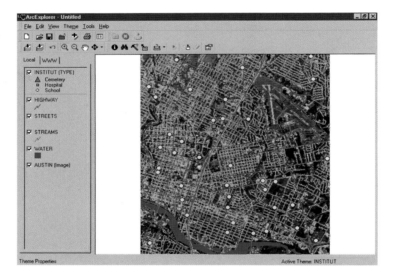

Your map is looking pretty good. All that remains is to add the coverage of flood areas to the map view.

**11**   Click the Add Theme button. Choose *ArcInfo Coverages* from the Data Types pull-down menu.

In the Add Theme(s) dialog box, navigate to the *flood* folder. Here you'll see a theme named pat.adf.

Click on the theme and then click Add Theme. The theme is added to the top of your legend as FLOOD.PAT.

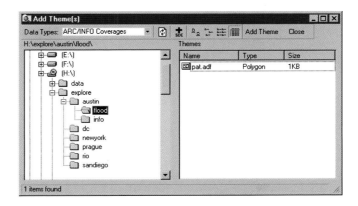

**12**   Turn on the FLOOD.PAT theme.

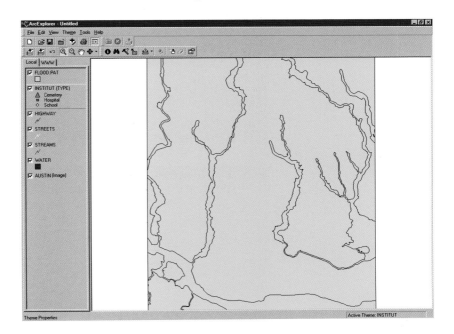

ArcExplorer displays themes in the order they appear in the legend, from bottom to top. Since the flood theme is on top of the list, it covers up all the other themes. You'll move it down the list a bit.

**13** Click on the name of the FLOOD.PAT theme in the legend and, holding down the mouse button, drag the mouse pointer down until it's between the AUSTIN (Image) and WATER themes, then release the mouse button.

Now you'll need to symbolize the FLOOD.PAT theme to show areas within a Special Flood Hazard Area (SFHA). These are areas expected to flood at least once within the next hundred years and are commonly called hundred-year flood zones.

Make the FLOOD.PAT theme active.

Click the Theme Properties button.

In the Theme Properties dialog box, select *Unique Values* under Classification Options.

Select *SFHA* as the field.

In the *Discrete values and symbols* section of the dialog box, you see that ArcExplorer automatically assigned random colors to each unique classification IN and OUT.

IN—Inside a hundred-year flood zone. Symbolize these areas in the map view as *green.*

OUT—Outside a hundred-year flood zone. Use a transparent symbol for this.

**14** Under *Discrete values and symbols,* click on the color box next to IN.

In the Symbol Properties dialog box, select *light green* for both the color and outline color, and *Dark gray fill* as the style. Click OK.

**15**  Under *Discrete values and symbols,* click on the color box next to OUT.

In the Symbol Properties dialog box, select *Transparent fill* as the style. Click OK. You needn't choose a color when the style is *Transparent fill.*

**16**  Click Remove Outline in the Theme Properties dialog box. Click OK.

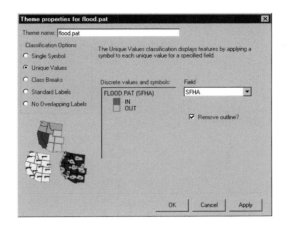

Your map view looks great. You know where you should be if you're ever in Austin and it starts to rain heavily. More importantly, you're prepared to use many different data types together if you ever need to. Now go ahead and explore your map. Use the pan and zoom tools to get a closer look, or use Identify and MapTips to see the names of streets, highways, streams, schools, and hospitals.

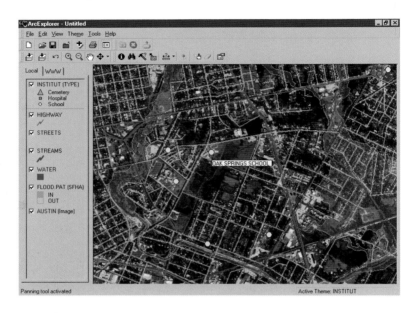

# *GIS for Everyone* companion CD

The *GIS for Everyone* CD–ROM includes more than 500 megabytes of digital geographic data for you to explore. The data covers features such as population, agriculture, income, economics, health, geological hazards (volcanoes and fault lines), roads, rivers, lakes, cities, forests, and mountain peaks.

Which files are used and how they're presented in a map is up to you. The result of these creative efforts might be something like the image shown below, made up of eleven different map layers. The order of the layers (from bottom to top), their colors, and the symbols used to represent each were selected after each layer was added. The final map image is in the hands of the mapmaker—you.

All the geographic data on the CD is located in the *data* and *explore* folders. These geographic files are listed and described in the CD's data dictionary in the file *DataDictionary.htm*. Each entry, organized to reflect the data directory structure, briefly describes the file's subject matter, geographic coverage, and date (if appropriate). Each entry also has a link to display information about all the attributes associated with each theme.

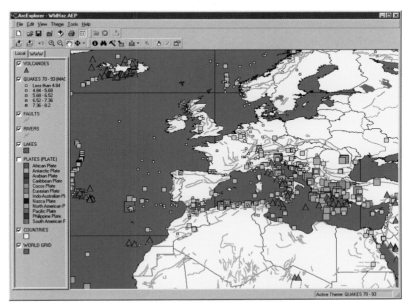

*This ArcExplorer project, showing world geologic hazards, lets you explore and analyze relationships among faults, earthquakes, volcanoes, and the earth's crustal plates.*

# Exploration 5-2   View data on the CD

We've included a couple of ArcExplorer projects to get you started exploring the data on the CD. These projects represent only a fraction of the possible things you can explore with the data.

1   Start ArcExplorer, if necessary.

2   Click the Open Project button. Navigate to the *data\aep* directory on the CD.

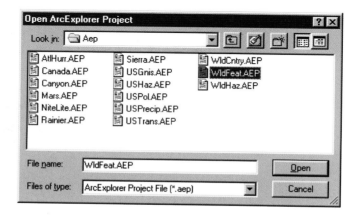

In the Open ArcExplorer Project dialog box, you see a lot of sample projects created from the data on the CD. Take a look at some of them.

**3**  Click on any of the .AEP files. The following table describes just a few of the available project files:

| Project | Description |
|---|---|
| AtlHurr.AEP | Explore the tracks of Atlantic hurricanes from 1886 to 1996. |
| Canada.AEP | Explore the natural and cultural features of Canada, including cities, national and provincial parks, aboriginal reservations, rivers and lakes, highways, and railroads. |
| Canyon.AEP | Explore a Sure!MAPS RASTER 1:100,000-scale topographic map of the Grand Canyon. |
| Mars.AEP | Explore an image of the surface of Mars. |
| NiteLite.AEP | Explore the nighttime lights over North America as seen from space. |
| Rainier.AEP | Explore a Sure!MAPS RASTER 1:100,000-scale topographic map of Mount Rainier National Park, Washington. |
| Sierra.AEP | Explore a Sure!MAPS RASTER 1:250,000-scale topographic map of the Sierra Nevada range, including 14,494-foot-high Mount Whitney. |
| USGnis.AEP | Explore the locations of physical and cultural geographic features throughout the United States and its territories, including buildings, cemeteries, churches, golf locales, hospitals, populated places, schools, and summits. |
| USHaz.AEP | Explore hazards within the United States, including earthquakes, hurricanes, and volcanoes. |
| USPol.AEP | Explore the 2000 presidential election results by state and representation by congressional district for the 107th and 108th congressional sessions. |
| USPrecip.AEP | Explore the average annual precipitation of the United States. |
| USTrans.AEP | Explore transportation between major U.S. urban areas including highways, rail, and airports. View the major time zones. |
| WldCntry.AEP | Explore world countries, including population, currency, major cities, time zones, and a gazetteer. |
| WldFeat.AEP | Explore world physical features such as rivers, lakes, and shaded relief. |
| WldHaz.AEP | Explore world geological features such as volcanoes, earthquakes and faults, and the location of the earth's crustal plates. |

These are just a few of the many projects you can create on your own using this data.

This map gives a vivid portrait of weather history, specifically 150 years of North Atlantic storm activity. The green tracks show the paths of subtropical depressions, tropical depressions, and major storms from 1851 to 2001, while the red tracks show major hurricanes that hit the United States during the same period, ending in 2000. Source: National Oceanic and Atmospheric Administration, National Hurricane Center.

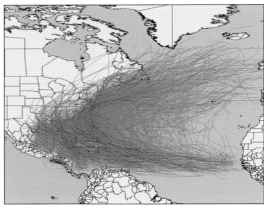

This map of the Korean peninsula shows important cities, as well as the proximity of the peninsula to its neighbors.

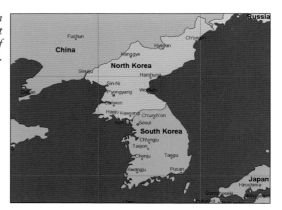

This satellite image shows what much of North America looks like at night from high above, with the brightest illumination coming from large urban population centers, while darkness envelops vast, less-populated stretches. The data was collected in 1996 and 1997 as part of the Defense Meteorological Satellite Program, and is courtesy of the National Geophysical Data Center.

# CHAPTER 6

# Bringing the world into your digital map

As in many other aspects of modern life, the Internet is having a profound, even revolutionary, effect on GIS. When connected through the Internet, geographic data is no longer confined to what can be stuffed into a hard drive or network server. Instead, digital data is becoming available twenty-four hours a day from sites everywhere around the globe. All this means that GIS mapping and analysis is becoming an even more dynamic process than it already was; for example, wireless personal digital assistants (PDAs) loaded with GIS software allow personnel working in emergency situations such as floods or wildfires to download real-time geographic data about weather conditions at the scene. Such a system is allowing for more flexible deployment of resources and quicker shifts in emergency-response tactics.

# Geography Network

Geography Network is a one-stop Internet shop of geographic data and services and more—a portal for geographic content distributed around the world, a place that is the first one where GIS users go for data. At the site, *www.geographynetwork.com,* a huge array of geographic content is available, including live maps, static maps, downloadable data, and map services. Because this content is delivered over the Internet, GIS professionals—and you—have access to the most up-to-date information available directly from the source.

You can think of Geography Network as a worldwide data bazaar, one that offers access to public-domain and other free data sources, as well as to many commercial data vendors; these commercial data sets can be accessed on a per-transaction basis, or by subscription. Some of the more popular types of geographic data you're likely to find include imagery, topography, demographics, boundaries, land use, land management, environmental, streets, weather, traffic, housing, and business.

**Types of Geography Network content**

Dynamic data and maps are live map services that you can use as a background display for use with your local data; you can also interact with the data online as if it were stored locally. The major advantage of these live maps is that you can access the most current data available without having to store any of that data on your system or maintain it over time.

*This map service published by Meteorlogix shows clouds and weather radar associated with Hurricane Lili as she made landfall in southern Louisiana in October 2002. Content title: Meteorlogix Weather Package (US).*

*Bringing the world into your digital map*

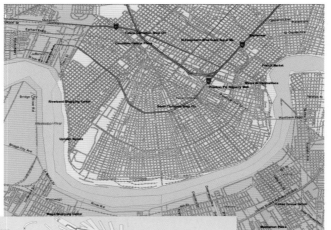

This map service published by ESRI presents a nation-wide street map based on the Census TIGER/Line 2000 data. The TIGER/Line® files are a digital database of geographic features, such as roads, railroads, rivers, lakes, political boundaries, census statistical boundaries, and so on, covering the United States. This map shows the city of New Orleans, Louisiana. Content title: TIGER 2000 Map Service.

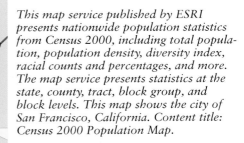

This map service published by ESRI presents nationwide population statistics from Census 2000, including total population, population density, diversity index, racial counts and percentages, and more. The map service presents statistics at the state, county, tract, block group, and block levels. This map shows the city of San Francisco, California. Content title: Census 2000 Population Map.

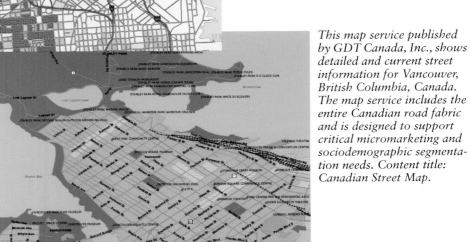

This map service published by GDT Canada, Inc., shows detailed and current street information for Vancouver, British Columbia, Canada. The map service includes the entire Canadian road fabric and is designed to support critical micromarketing and sociodemographic segmentation needs. Content title: Canadian Street Map.

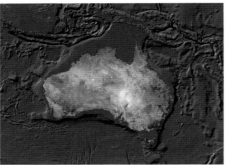

*This map service shows a portion of WorldSat's 1-kilometer-resolution, georeferenced, cloud-free, full-Earth data set, collected and processed from the National Oceanographic and Atmospheric Administration's series of weather satellites. These Advanced Very High Resolution Radiometers (AVHRR) orbit the earth at an altitude of 820 kilometers (520 miles) and above. This data is useful as a basemap for GIS applications. Map service title: Satellite Imagery (1K).*

*This map service published by DigitalGlobe shows a natural color image of the three Pyramids of Giza, near Cairo, Egypt, taken February 2, 2002, from the DigitalGlobe Quickbird Satellite orbiting at 450 kilometers above the earth's surface. Satellite imagery is commonly used in many GIS applications. Content title: Pyramids of Giza, Egypt - February 2, 2002.*

The technology behind these live maps is ArcIMS, an Internet mapping solution created by ESRI. These live maps are delivered in one of two ways: an image service or a feature service. It's important to know the difference:

- An image map service allows you to incorporate a background map to your existing data. An image map service works by taking a snapshot of a map on a server computer and delivering it to your GIS as an image. A new, updated map image is generated each time the client computer (you) requests new information. With an image map service, you can obtain information about individual features, and you can pan and zoom throughout the entire map.

- A feature map service streams compressed vector features directly to your GIS. Feature streaming enables more advanced tasks on the client computer, such as feature labeling, feature symbolization, creation of Map Tips, and selection of features. As with an image map service, you can also obtain feature information and pan and zoom throughout the entire map.

Downloadable data is geographic data sets that may be downloaded for immediate use with your GIS software. Often, you can customize the download to a specific area you are previewing. Some data may be downloaded for free, while other data may be ordered through a simple e-commerce transaction.

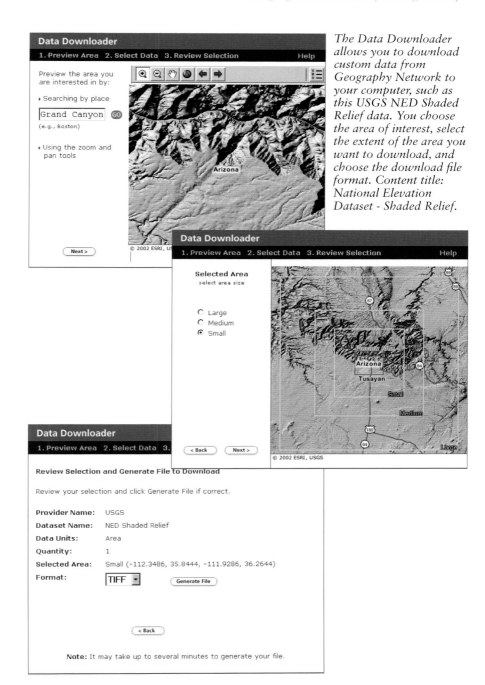

The Data Downloader
allows you to download
custom data from
Geography Network to
your computer, such as
this USGS NED Shaded
Relief data. You choose
the area of interest, select
the extent of the area you
want to download, and
choose the download file
format. Content title:
National Elevation
Dataset - Shaded Relief.

Data clearinghouses are usually Web sites maintained by organizations and companies that handle specific types of information. The data may be categorized by geographic region, department, project, or content, or by the digital characteristics of the data itself. This data can be downloaded and added to your GIS to use with your existing data. Data clearinghouses can be very comprehensive, so you should know what you are looking for.

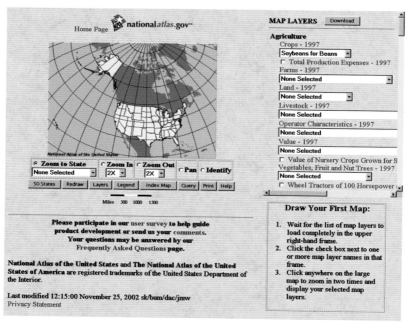

*At the Web site of the National Atlas of the United States, a service of the U.S. Department of the Interior, drop-down boxes let you choose from a wide array of U.S. data sets—ranging from agriculture to geology to demographics to epidemiology—and combine them for specific areas of the country.*

GIS applications are increasingly being deployed on the Internet. Applications are GIS-enabled, custom Web-based or desktop applications built to support consumers of geographic information. These applications are supported using Geography Network content and Web services. The applications are usually geared toward a particular audience and might include map services in the background for reference, or functionality such as address matching, routing, proximity, and mapping. Such interactive mapping sites allow you to create maps without GIS software. You connect to the Web site using your Web browser and build your map while you are online. For example, you might create a map of driving directions, or find out where a house is located from an online real estate listing.

Bringing the world into your digital map

*The National Geographic MapMachine (www.nationalgeographic.com/mapmachine) is an interactive mapping site that allows you to access a wide variety of geographic information covering the world, such as this atlas map of Iraq. The MapMachine offers dynamic maps from many of the world's leading data providers, atlas maps from the* National Geographic Seventh Edition Atlas, *and flags and facts information for countries and states. The MapMachine is powered by ESRI Internet mapping technology and built on content from Geography Network.*

**Tools for accessing Geography Network content**

There are several tools to help you access all the content Geography Network has to offer. You can use the ArcExplorer software you are already familiar with, as well as Geography Network Explorer, ArcExplorer Web Services Edition, or a full software visualization and analysis package such as ArcGIS.

Geography Network Explorer offers a straightforward browser interface that lets you search, browse, and preview the metadata of content found on Geography Network. Metadata is simply information about the data you are using, and describes the content, quality, condition, provenance, and other characteristics of the data. With the Explorer, you can search by geographic extent, content type, content theme, or keyword, or you can simply browse through all available metadata documents. The metadata you find will help you decide if the data it describes best fits your needs.

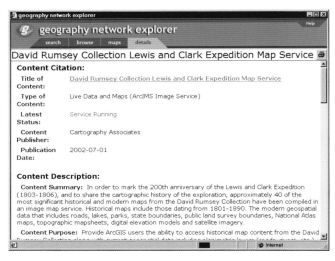

*Use the Geography Network Explorer to find and preview content on Geography Network such as this map that celebrates the 200th anniversary of the Lewis and Clark Expedition. You can use the Details tab to read full content description and access information and use the Maps tab to preview and explore the map using standard navigation tools. Content title: David Rumsey Collection Lewis and Clark Expedition Map Service.*

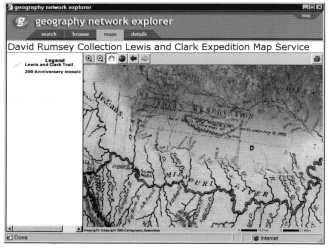

ArcExplorer Web is a fully functional GIS interface developed with ArcIMS. This tool, which looks a great deal like the ArcExplorer software you've been using up until now, allows you to perform basic GIS analysis of selected data through the browser, but without downloading any special viewing software or other plug-in software. It includes standard mapping tools, such as zoom, pan, identify, and find. Not only does ArcExplorer Web allow you to access an individual map service, but you can also display multiple map services together using a transparency function. You can also save a link to your map for easy access in the future, or create a link to your map for inclusion on your own page.

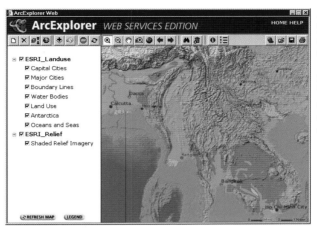

*ArcExplorer Web allows you to simultaneously explore multiple dynamic map services in your Web browser without the need for plug-ins. This map combines separate map services of land use and shaded relief. Content titles: World Landuse Zones, World Shaded Relief.*

ArcExplorer 4 Java™ Edition is similar to the ArcExplorer 2 software you've used thus far. But the Java version lets you search for and explore maps and other data on Geography Network via a direct connection to Geography Network Explorer. Once you find data that may be interesting, you can read a description of it, preview it over the Internet, and immediately integrate this data in ArcExplorer with your local data.

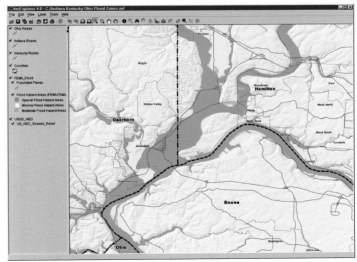

*ArcExplorer Java allows you to integrate remote data in the form of map services with local data you already have. This map of the tri-state area of Ohio, Kentucky, and Indiana shows local data of county boundaries and roads combined with remote data of FEMA flood polygons and shaded relief. Content titles: U.S. Flood Risk Zones, National Elevation Dataset - Shaded Relief.*

You should install ArcExplorer 4 Java Edition now to use this feature in the next exploration.

### INSTALL ARCEXPLORER 4 JAVA EDITION

To run ArcExplorer, you must have Microsoft Windows 98, Windows 2000, Windows NT, or Windows XP for Intel® installed on your system, Service Pack 4, 5, or 6a (6a is recommended).

To install ArcExplorer,

1 Insert the *GIS for Everyone* CD in your CD–ROM drive.

2 Choose Run from the Start menu.

3 In the Command Line box, type the letter of your CD–ROM drive, a colon, a backslash, the directory path Software\AE4Java, a backslash, and the file name AEJavaSetup.exe (for example, **E:\Software\AE4Java\AEJavaSetup.exe**).

4 Follow the on-screen instructions to complete the installation.

ArcExplorer 4 Java Edition requires that the Java Runtime Environment (also known as the Java Runtime, or JRE) be present. If you don't have this software already installed, the setup program will prompt you to install it. This file is named j2re-1_3_1-win-i.exe and is also located on the *GIS for Everyone* CD in the Ae4Java directory (for example, **E:\software\AE4Java\ j2re-1_3_1-win-i.exe**).

# Exploration 6-1    Explore giant sequoia groves using data from Geography Network

Photo by David Davis

In this exploration, you'll use ArcExplorer 4 to find data on Geography Network and then use it simultaneously with data that you already have. Keep in mind that because Geography Network's map services are delivered over the Internet, your computer's performance during this exercise will vary according to the speed of your connection. This exercise is also available online at *www.esri.com/gisforeveryone/sequoia.htm*. Because Geography Network itself is dynamic, the steps will be updated there as needed.

Assume you are a tour organizer in Europe specializing in environmentally friendly tours of the United States. Your customers are young and active, interested in outdoor vacation activities, and attracted to the natural wonders of North America rather than its monuments and museums. You want to introduce this clientele to the giant sequoia *(Sequoiadendron giganteum)* groves of central California, and so you have organized a tour of Sequoia and Kings Canyon National Parks in the Sierra Nevada mountain range. Because your clientele is intelligent and curious, you'll show them some digital maps of the area where they want to do some serious hiking. These maps illustrate various natural phenomena in the park areas, including the areas where these magnificent trees grow best. You want your clientele to understand the spatial patterns between giant sequoia grove location, elevation, precipitation, and location on the windward (wet) and lee (dry) sides of a mountain range.

You already have data from the U.S. National Park Service showing the park boundaries, giant sequoia grove locations, and trails. What you don't have is topographic and precipitation data. Since you will also be leading the hikes up to see the trees, you're also going to need some road data. You turn to Geography Network for help in finding this other important data.

**1**  Start ArcExplorer 4 Java Edition.

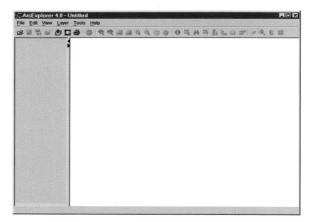

**2**  Click the Add Layers button. The Catalog dialog box displays.

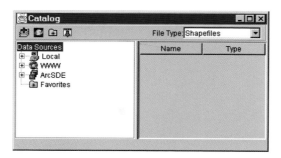

This dialog box works just like the Add Theme(s) dialog box you used in the Austin exercise, but notice that there are Local, WWW, and ArcSDE® Data Sources listed. You'll be able to view data from all over the world from here.

**3** On the left side of the Catalog dialog box, click the plus sign next to Local and find your CD drive. Then go to the *explore\sequoia* directory on the CD.

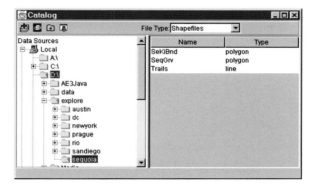

When you open the *sequoia* directory, you'll see three shapefiles. The first, *SeKiBnd,* contains the boundary lines for Sequoia and Kings Canyon National Parks. The next, *SeqGrv,* contains the location of all giant sequoia groves within the two parks' boundaries. The last, *Trails,* contains the location of all maintained hiking trails within the parks. You'll add the first two files to your map now, and the third one later.

**4** On the right side of the Catalog dialog box, click *SeKiBnd.* In the Catalog dialog box, click the Add Layers button, then *SeqGrv,* and then the Add Layers button. When the layers are added, close the Catalog dialog box.

**5** Turn on the two new layers in the legend.

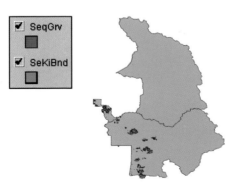

You'll probably need to assign more appropriate symbols to represent the layers.

**6** Double-click the *SeKiBnd* layer in the legend. The SeKiBnd Properties dialog box appears.

For Style, choose *Transparent fill.*

Under Outline, choose *Dash line* as the Style, make sure *Blue* is chosen for Color, and set the Width to *2*.

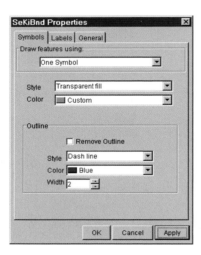

Click the General Tab. Change the Layer Name to *Park Boundaries.*

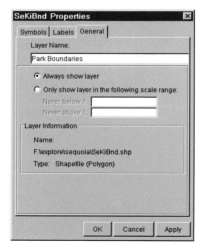

*Bringing the world into your digital map*

Click OK.

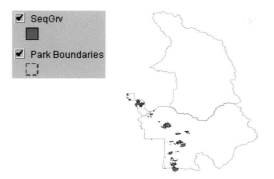

**7** Double-click the *SeqGrv* layer in the legend to display the SeqGrv Properties dialog box.

For Color, choose *<Custom>*. The Color Chooser dialog box appears.

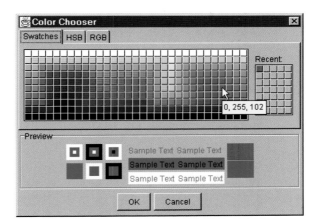

Click on a light green color box of your choice and click OK.

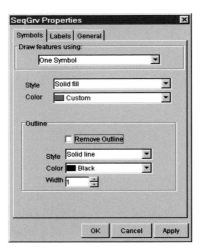

Click the General Tab. Change the Layer Name to *Giant Sequoia Groves.*

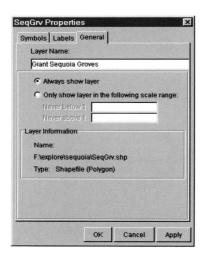

Click OK.

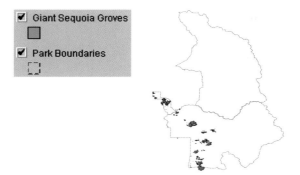

Now that you can see the location of the giant sequoia groves within the parks, you're ready to look for data showing the mountains.

**8** Click the Geography Network button. The Geography Network Explorer opens in your Web browser window. A Search tab and a Browse tab are at the top. By default, the Search tab is active.

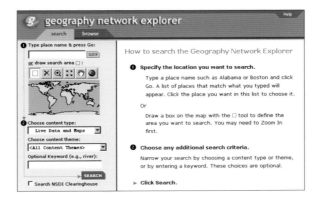

You use the Search tab to search for data by geographic area. The Browse tab is used for searching for data by data publisher or type of data. You are interested in Sequoia National Park, so you'll start with a geographic search.

**9** To find data, you must follow first step 1 and then 2. In the step 1 text box, type **Sequoia National Park** and then click Go.

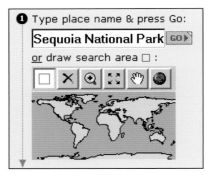

A matching place-name is found.

**10** Click *Sequoia National Park, California, United States.*

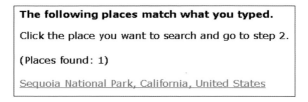

The locator map zooms to the search area.

Now that your search area is defined, your next task is to define your search criteria—to tell Geography Network that you are looking specifically for elevation data for the geographic area you have chosen.

**11** Under the locator map, leave the content type set to *Live Data and Maps.* Change the content theme in the box below to *Elevation and Derived Prods.* In the Optional Keyword box, type **Elevation**. Click Search at the bottom of the Find Content area.

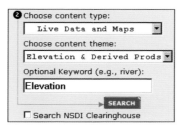

A number of different maps are found. The one you will use in this exercise is called National Elevation Dataset - Shaded Relief and is published by the U.S. Geological Survey. It should be the third one in the list. (If it isn't, scroll until you locate it.)

Below each map are buttons that let you see additional details about the data, view a larger version of the map, or add the map to ArcExplorer.

**12** Click the View Details button under the National Elevation Dataset - Shaded Relief content listing.

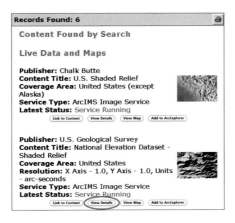

Scroll through the details page. There is information about the map's content, its spatial properties, and the restrictions on its use. Of interest to you is the content purpose, which tells you that the map has the shaded relief content you are looking for, and that it is useful for geographic reference, or for a background image.

> **Content Description:**
>
> **Content Summary:** The USGS National Elevation Dataset (NED) has been developed by merging the highest-resolution, best-quality elevation data available across the United States into a seamless raster format. NED is the result of the maturation of the USGS effort to provide 1:24,000-scale Digital Elevation Model (DEM) data for the conterminous US and 1:63,360-scale DEM data for Alaska. The shaded relief display is derived from NED using a hill-shade technique.
>
> **Content Purpose:** The primary purpose for a shaded relief display is for geographic reference, or for a background image. Another purpose is to enhance topographic structure that is perpendicular to the illumination angle. In this case, the illumination is from the Northwest to the Southeast.

**13** Click the Maps tab above the details page.

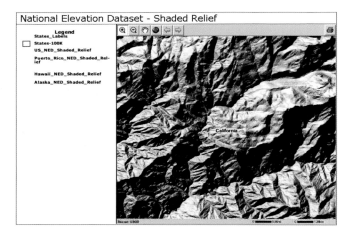

The map shows elevation in relief for your search area of Sequoia National Park. The map has everything you are looking for. If you like, use the navigation buttons above the map to explore the data further.

To use this data over the Internet simultaneously with the Sequoia Groves and Park Boundaries data that is already on your computer, you simply need to add it from this location.

**14** Click the Details tab, scroll down to the bottom of the Access and Usage Information section, and Click the Add to ArcExplorer button.

If you like, you can minimize the Geography Network Explorer window. Don't close it though, because you'll be using it again shortly.

**15** Now go back to the ArcExplorer 4 window.

A new live map named USGS_GN_NED is added to the top of your legend. Click the check box next to the name USGS_GN_NED in the legend to turn on the map service. The check box will blink green, which means that the map is loading from the Geography Network servers. After a moment, the shaded relief map is displayed.

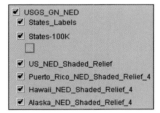

What you have loaded is not the data itself, but an image service. Any instructions that you give to ArcExplorer (such as zooming or turning layers on or off) are relayed through the Internet to a remote server where the data is stored. This computer carries out the operation and sends an image of the result back to you.

The map service contains a series of sublayers: *States_Labels, States_100K* (or *States_2M*), *US_NED_Shaded_Relief,* and so on. You don't want the states labeled so you'll turn that sublayer off.

**16**  Uncheck the *States_Labels* sublayer in the legend.

**17**  To make room in the legend, right-click the name *US_NED_Shaded_Relief* in the legend and uncheck *Display Layer Classification.*

Since this map service covers your original two data layers, you'll need to move it to the bottom of the Table of Contents.

**18**  Right-click the name *USGS_GN_NED* in the legend, click *Move Layer,* then click *Move to Bottom.*

The boundary lines are hard to see against the dark background of the shaded relief map. You'll lighten the shaded relief map by increasing its transparency.

**19**  Double-click the name *USGS_GN_NED* in the legend to display the USGS_GN_NED Properties dialog box. Slide the Transparency bar to the right so that it is set to *60%*.

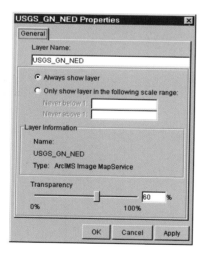

Click OK.

Now you can see the national park boundaries and the giant sequoia grove locations in relation to the mountains. You can now show this to your clients, pointing out that the natural range of the giant sequoias occurs on the western side of the Sierra Nevada range.

You'll save this map as an image file to include on your Web site, and to send in an e-mail to tour participants.

**20**   From the Edit menu, choose Copy Map Image to File. Navigate to a directory location of your choice. Name the file *Central_Sierra.jpg* and click Save.

While the map shows that sequoias grow in the mountains, it doesn't allow you to see at which elevation these trees grow, and therefore, how high you and your clients will have to climb to see them. Again, you'll use Geography Network to find the data to do this.

**21**   Open the Geography Network Explorer window. Click the Search tab if necessary.

Change the Optional Keyword to *Elevation Zones.*

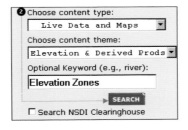

Click Search.

The map you are interested in is called Elevation and Precipitation Zones and is published by ESRI Press.

**Publisher:** ESRI Press
**Content Title:** Elevation and Precipitation Zones
**Coverage Area:** Sequoia and Kings Canyon National Park
**Service Type:** ArcIMS Image Service
**Latest Status:** Service Running

( Link to Content )   ( View Details )   ( View Map )   ( Add to ArcExplorer )

**22**   In Geography Network Explorer, preview the map and its description. When you are finished exploring the data, add it to ArcExplorer and turn on the EDU_Sequoia map service.

You can minimize the Geography Network Explorer window, but don't close it.

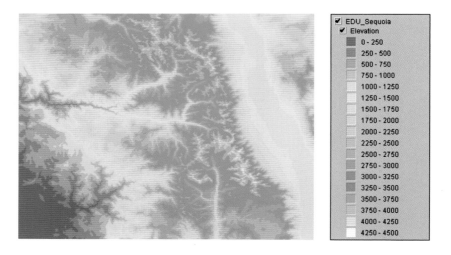

The new live map is added to the top of your legend and the elevation zones are displayed. You'll move it down in the Table of Contents so it will work better with the other layers.

**23** Right-click the name *EDU_SEQUOIA* in the legend, click *Move Layer*, then click *Move Down*. Repeat this action until the EDU_SEQUOIA layer is just above the USGS_GN_NED layer.

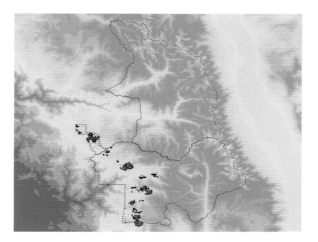

This map shows elevation zones by shaded colors. The green and yellow colors show lower elevation, while the orange, purple, and white colors show higher elevation.

Since the EDU_SEQUOIA layer obscures the USGS_GN_NED layer, you'll set the transparency of the EDU_SEQUOIA layer so that you and your clients can see the mountains beneath.

**24** Double-click the name *EDU_SEQUOIA* in the legend to display the EDU_SEQUOIA Properties dialog box. Slide the Transparency bar to the right to *50%*.

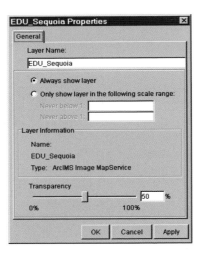

Click OK.

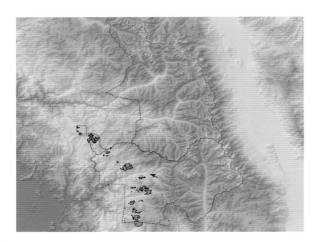

You have just created a color shaded relief map, which shows the elevation combined with the relief. This combination creates an attractive overall map that shows both mountain heights and surface shapes.

With this map, your clients are ready to find out at what elevations giant sequoias grow best.

**25** Make the Giant Sequoia Groves layer active in the Legend and then click the Zoom to Active Layer button.

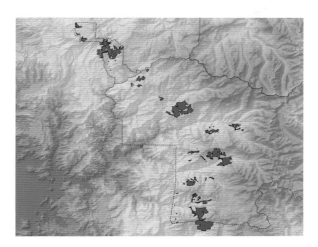

When the map zooms in, you take a closer look at the groves within the two parks.

 **26** Make the Elevation layer active and click the Identify button. Click within some of the giant sequoia grove locations.

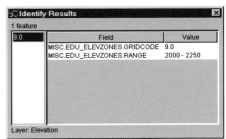

The Identify Results dialog box shows several attributes. You're interested in the *RANGE* attribute, which tells you the elevation range in meters of each grove you click on.

Your clients will find that the elevations of the sequoia groves generally range from 1,000 to 2,750 meters, with the majority occurring at about the middle of these two extremes.

If you like, save this map as an image file named *Sequoia_Elevzones.jpg* to a directory of your choice.

**27**  Turn off the Elevation layer and turn on the Precipitation layer.

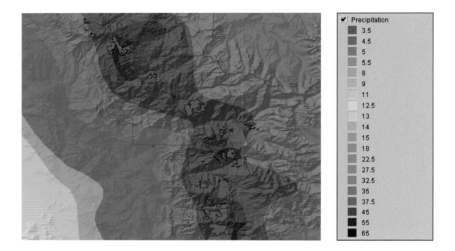

This map shows annual rain or snowfall in inches, by shaded colors. The yellow and orange colors show lower totals, while the dark blue colors show higher.

You can use this map to find out how much precipitation falls in areas that contain giant sequoias.

**28**  Make the Precipitation layer active and make sure the Identify tool is still selected. Again, click within the giant sequoia groves.

 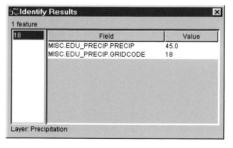

Your clients will find that sequoias are found in areas that receive a mean annual rainfall or snowfall total of between 35 to 55 inches.

If you like, save this map as an image file named *Sequoia_Precipitation.jpg* to a directory of your choice.

You now know that giant sequoias grow in a few scattered pockets along a narrow band on the western Sierra Nevada slopes of California, and that they have specific elevation and precipitation requirements. To cap off your study, you'll determine just how narrow this band is.

**29** Click the Measure tool and choose *Miles* as the distance unit.

**30** Click and hold your mouse button as you drag a line segment across the imaginary rectangle containing the sequoia band, using the image below as your guide. Release the mouse button at the end of the segment.

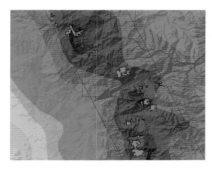

You should see that giant sequoias occur in a narrow band about 15 miles wide within the parks.

**31** Turn off the EDU_Sequoia map service.

**32** Right-click the name *EDU_Sequoia* in the legend and uncheck Display Layer Classification.

**33** Right-click the name *Park Boundaries* in the legend and Click Zoom to Active Layer.

Now that your analysis is complete, you'll make a map that you and your clients can use to plan the trip to Sequoia National Park. You'll see if you can find some roads data on Geography Network.

**34** Open the Geography Network Explorer Window. Click the Search tab if necessary.

Make sure the step 1 box still shows Sequoia National Park and the locator map. Change the content theme in step 2 to *<All Content Themes>* and change the optional keyword to *Transportation Data.*

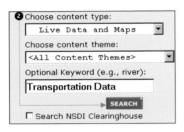

Click Search.

The map you are interested in is called TIGER 2000 Map Service and is published by ESRI. TIGER 2000 is data created and maintained by the U.S. Bureau of the Census. It is free and works well for making basemaps.

Add this map to ArcExplorer and close Geography Network Explorer.

Turn on the new Census_TIGER2000 map service.

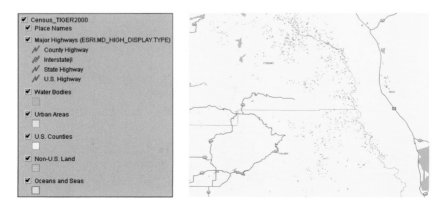

A map service named Census_TIGER2000 is added to your legend. Move this layer down in the legend so that it is below Park Boundaries and above EDU_Sequoia.

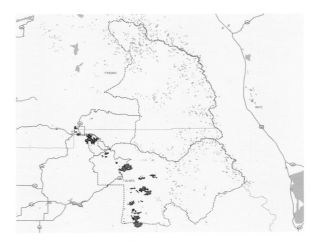

The map shows features such as place-names, major highways, and water bodies.

Now you'll enhance this map with the shaded relief.

**35**  Double-click the name *Census_TIGER2000* in the legend to display the Census_TIGER2000 Properties dialog box.

Change the transparency to *50%*.

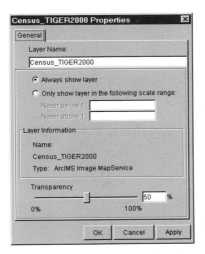

Click OK.

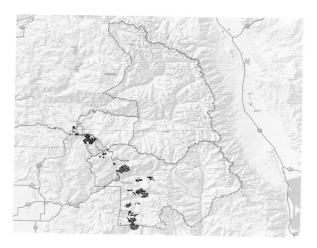

As a final touch to your map, you'll add and symbolize the trails layer that you obtained from the National Park Service.

**36** Click the Add Layers button to display the Catalog dialog.

Add the Trails shapefile from your *explore\sequoia* directory on the CD.

Turn on the Trails layer. Double-click the Trails layer in the legend to display the Trails Properties dialog box.

For Style, choose *Dash line* and choose *Dark Gray* as the Color.

Click OK.

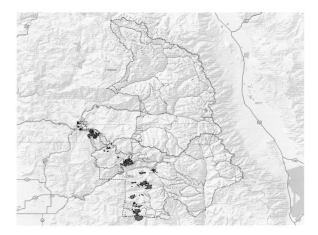

**37**  You can use the MapTips or Identify tools to discover the names of anything on the map, such as roads, lakes, or sequoia groves.

If you want to save your work, click the File menu and click Save Project.
Navigate to a directory location of your choice. Name the file *Sequoia.axl*
and click Save.

If you save the map, when you reopen it, ArcExplorer will automatically
load the map service, as long as your Internet connection is active. If your
connection is not active, ArcExplorer will inform you that it can't locate the
source data.

Your map is complete. You and your clients are well prepared for a successful
tour of one of America's greatest national treasures.

# Geographic information elsewhere on the Internet

While the amount of data you can find on Geography Network may seem immense, far more is available elsewhere on the Internet. More and more national, regional, and local government agencies are making data available, either for download or for exploration online through interactive mapping tools such as ArcIMS.

Search engines are probably the best starting point for locating this geographic data. Begin your search by accessing your favorite search engine, such as Google (www.google.com), Excite (www.excite.com), and Yahoo (www.yahoo.com). Different search engines will locate different sites, and each engine has its own features, so it pays to try them all to find those that suit you.

Try using combinations of keywords related to the specific data you're looking for. Include search terms that indicate that you're looking for digital geographic data, such as "GIS data" or "spatial data." Include search terms that specify the particular geographic area of interest. You can also narrow your search by including specific formats, such as "shapefile" or "DRG." Use different combinations of these search terms.

You'll wind up with many links to explore. Perhaps the most useful sites are those that specialize in providing collections of links to sites offering GIS data to download. You'll also find the Web pages of federal, state, and local government agencies, many of which offer free downloadable data. Academic and commercial data providers will also turn up.

**GIS for Everyone Web site**

If you enjoyed creating maps in the explorations and want to learn more about GIS and all it has to offer, be sure to pay a visit to the *GIS for Everyone* Web site at *www.esri.com/gisforeveryone.*

Links from this page will let you:

- Update the giant sequoia exploration
- Learn the basic theory behind GIS
- Learn how you can make GIS a career
- Find additional GIS training
- Learn about more powerful GIS software
- Find additional geographic data sources

# Exploration 6-2    Download data for a U.S. ZIP Code

As a bonus for buying this book, you can access data for your own neighborhood, or for any area in the United States, using the special access code inside the back cover. You'll receive up to three themes for your selected area, depending upon availability, including GDT streets data, FEMA flood data, and census data.

The data will be provided to you as a compressed file you can download to your local computer and then drag and drop into ArcExplorer.

1  Using your Web browser, access the *GIS for Everyone* Web site at *www.esri.com/gisforeveryone.*

2  Access the Download Data for your Neighborhood link to display the download form.

| **Download GIS Neighborhood Data** |
| --- |
| 1. Full Name: |
| 2. E-mail Address: |
| 3. User Access Code: |
| 4. Neighborhood ZIP Code:   (5-digit [e.g., 92373]) |
| Submit Request |

3  Enter your name, the fourteen-digit access code inside the back cover of this book, and the ZIP Code for which you want to download data. Be sure you enter the ZIP Code digits accurately; you can only do this once.

If you're outside the United States or don't have a specific ZIP Code you wish to download, several sample data sets are available to download from this page.

4  Click the Download button to process your request. It may take a few moments for your data file to be created.

5  When your file is ready, you'll be given a link from which you can download a compressed file containing the available themes of streets, flood zones, and census statistics.

Download the file and save it in a directory you've created on your PC (for example, *C:\homedata*).

Bringing the world into your digital map

Now you can add your themes to ArcExplorer.

**6**   Start ArcExplorer, if necessary.

ArcExplorer™

**7**   Using Windows Explorer, drag and drop the downloaded file into the ArcExplorer window. When prompted, save the data in the same directory as the Zip file (e.g., *C:\homedata*). Since it has a *default.AEP* file, all the themes are added to your map view automatically. The streets data and flood data is turned on for you.

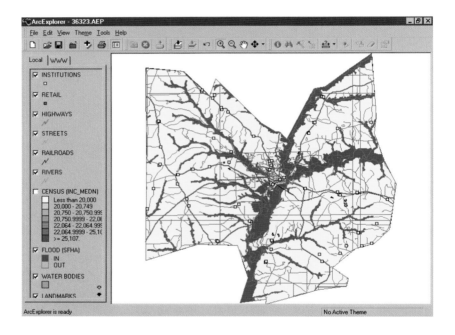

**8** Now turn off the FLOOD theme. Turn on the CENSUS theme. It's symbolized according to income. Use this theme's other attributes to learn about the people in your community.

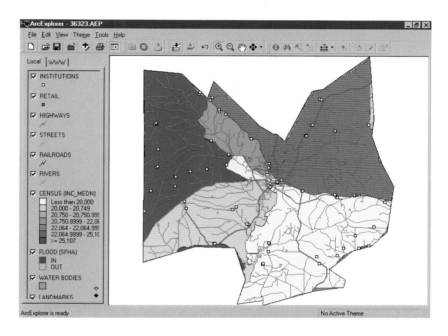

Be sure to check the *GIS for Everyone* Web site for other data sets in your area of interest that are available for downloading.

# *Data compatibility*

CREATING DIGITAL MAPS often requires bringing together data from a wide variety of sources. It's important that you know as much as you can about the sources of your data, for several reasons. Two chief reasons involve map projection and map scale.

**Themes must be of the same map projection**

The earth's surface is curved, but maps are flat. To represent three-dimensional space on a two-dimensional surface, a mathematical transformation called a *projection* is used. Many different map projections exist to support a wide variety of uses; maps that you've seen hanging on the walls of classrooms are frequently in the Mercator projection. Projections are all distinguished by their ability to represent a particular portion of the earth's surface. A projection that gives an accurate depiction of one portion of the globe may not work for a different portion. For example, the Mercator projection is good for depicting the earth's surface at the equator, but at the cost of distorting features near the north and south poles. This is why Greenland looks bigger than it actually is on Mercator-projection maps.

If you're working with multiple data themes in ArcExplorer, they must all be in the same projection for you to be able to see them together. If they're not, they won't show up in the same view. If you have problems with this, the best thing to do is to find out from the source of the data whether the information is available in the map projection that suits your needs. You can often find out which type of map projection you're working with from the place you get the data. If you get it from a Web site, the projection will most likely be listed with its description, or in a readme file stored with the data.

**Themes must be of the appropriate scale**

In order to represent a portion of the earth's surface on a map, the area must obviously be reduced. This reduction is called map *scale*. It's defined as the ratio of map distance to ground distance, and is commonly expressed as a ratio or a fraction, such as 1:24,000.

The values on either side of the colon in this fraction represent the proportion between distance on the map and distance on the ground in the same units. For example, "1:24,000" means "1 map inch represents 24,000 ground inches," or "1 map meter represents 24,000 ground meters."

In general, small-scale maps depict large ground areas, but they show little detail. On the other hand, large-scale maps depict small ground areas, but show much greater detail. The features on small-scale maps more closely represent real-world features, because the extent of reduction is lower than that of large-scale maps. As map scale decreases, features must be smoothed and simplified, or not shown at all. In other words, a dime-sized lake on a large-scale map (1:1,200) would be less than the size of the period at the end of this sentence on a small-scale map (1:1,000,000).

Every data set is designed for display at a particular scale (or within a range of scales). For example, a 1:500,000 data set will look "right" when displayed at that scale, but will look too sketchy if displayed at 1:50,000. If displayed at 1:5,000,000, it will look too "busy" or crowded and will take too long to draw on the monitor. If you find themes from multiple sources, be sure they're compatible. Data gathered for display at 1:1,000,000 shouldn't be displayed with 1:10,000-scale data.

# IMPORT71

A COMMON DATA FORMAT available on the Internet that you can use in ArcExplorer is the ArcInfo coverage. However, coverages are frequently in a portable format, E00, that you have to convert before you can display in your ArcExplorer project. The tool to do this, the IMPORT71 utility, is included on the CD.

### INSTALL IMPORT71

1 Insert the *GIS for Everyone* CD in your CD–ROM drive.

2 Choose Run from the Start menu.

3 In the Command Line box, type the letter of your CD–ROM drive, a colon, a backslash, and import71.exe (for example, **E:\import71.exe**).

4 Either accept the default location to install IMPORT71, C:\Program Files\ESRI\Import71, or choose another one. Then click Next.

5 On the next screen, click Finish. When asked if you want to add a shortcut for this program to your desktop, choose Yes.

# To use IMPORT71

Import71

**1** Click on the IMPORT71 Utility icon on your desktop to bring up its dialog box.

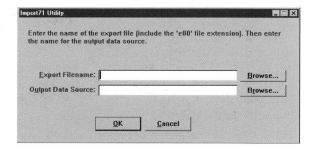

The Export Filename is simply the full name and path of the .e00 file you wish to convert to a coverage, for example *H:\data\flood.e00*. You can type the location in but it's often easier to use the Browse button.

**2** Click the Browse button to locate the .e00 file.

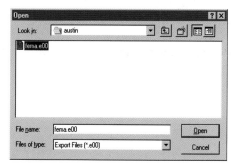

You need to use your PC's file management system to create a folder in which to store the coverage you'll create.

**3** Using a program like Windows Explorer, create a new folder on your computer to store the coverage.

**4** Type in the full path to your output data source. If you call the coverage *flood*, your path might be *C:\data\flood*.

You can also use the Browse button to choose the Windows Explorer directory to store the new imported coverage in, but you'll still need to enter a file
name. Browse only lets you pick the directory to store it in.

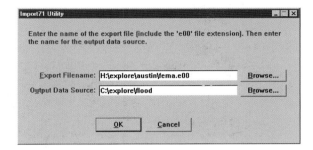

**5**  When both values are filled in, click OK. The IMPORT71 Utility will import
the .e00 file and create a coverage. It will inform you when it has finished.

Once the file has been imported, you can add it to your map view.